Reallotment

BRITANNICA
Mathematics
in
Context

Geometry and Measurement

TEACHER'S GUIDE

HOLT, RINEHART AND WINSTON

Mathematics in Context is a comprehensive curriculum for the middle grades.
It was developed in 1991 through 1997 in collaboration with the Wisconsin Center
for Education Research, School of Education, University of Wisconsin-Madison and
the Freudenthal Institute at the University of Utrecht, The Netherlands, with the
support of the National Science Foundation Grant No. 9054928.

The revision of the curriculum was carried out in 2003 through 2005, with the
support of the National Science Foundation Grant No. ESI 0137414.

National Science Foundation
Opinions expressed are those of the authors
and not necessarily those of the Foundation.

Gravemeijer, K.; Abels, M.; Wijers, M.; Pligge, M. A.; Clarke, B.; and Burrill, G.
(2006). *Reallotment.* In Wisconsin Center for Education Research & Freudenthal
Institute (Eds.), *Mathematics in context.* Chicago: Encyclopædia Britannica.

The Teacher's Guide for this unit was prepared by David C. Webb, Candace Ulmer,
Mieke Abels, and Truus Dekker.

ISBN 0-03-039803-7

2 3 4 5 6 073 09 08 07 06

The *Mathematics in Context* Development Team

Development 1991–1997

The initial version of *Reallotment* was developed by Koeno Gravemeijer. It was adapted for use in American schools by Margaret A. Pligge and Barbara Clarke.

Wisconsin Center for Education

Research Staff

Thomas A. Romberg
Director

Joan Daniels Pedro
Assistant to the Director

Gail Burrill
Coordinator

Margaret R. Meyer
Coordinator

Project Staff

Jonathan Brendefur
Laura Brinker
James Browne
Jack Burrill
Rose Byrd
Peter Christiansen
Barbara Clarke
Doug Clarke
Beth R. Cole
Fae Dremock
Mary Ann Fix

Sherian Foster
James A, Middleton
Jasmina Milinkovic
Margaret A. Pligge
Mary C. Shafer
Julia A. Shew
Aaron N. Simon
Marvin Smith
Stephanie Z. Smith
Mary S. Spence

Freudenthal Institute Staff

Jan de Lange
Director

Els Feijs
Coordinator

Martin van Reeuwijk
Coordinator

Mieke Abels
Nina Boswinkel
Frans van Galen
Koeno Gravemeijer
Marja van den Heuvel-Panhuizen
Jan Auke de Jong
Vincent Jonker
Ronald Keijzer
Martin Kindt

Jansie Niehaus
Nanda Querelle
Anton Roodhardt
Leen Streefland
Adri Treffers
Monica Wijers
Astrid de Wild

Revision 2003–2005

The revised version of *Reallotment* was developed by Mieke Abels and Monica Wijers. It was adapted for use in American schools by Gail Burrill.

Wisconsin Center for Education

Research Staff

Thomas A. Romberg
Director

David C. Webb
Coordinator

Gail Burrill
Editorial Coordinator

Margaret A. Pligge
Editorial Coordinator

Project Staff

Sarah Ailts
Beth R. Cole
Erin Hazlett
Teri Hedges
Karen Hoiberg
Carrie Johnson
Jean Krusi
Elaine McGrath

Margaret R. Meyer
Anne Park
Bryna Rappaport
Kathleen A. Steele
Ana C. Stephens
Candace Ulmer
Jill Vettrus

Freudenthal Institute Staff

Jan de Lange
Director

Truus Dekker
Coordinator

Mieke Abels
Content Coordinator

Monica Wijers
Content Coordinator

Arthur Bakker
Peter Boon
Els Feijs
Dédé de Haan
Martin Kindt

Nathalie Kuijpers
Huub Nilwik
Sonia Palha
Nanda Querelle
Martin van Reeuwijk

Cover photo credits: (left to right) © Comstock Images; © Corbis; © Getty Images

Illustrations
x Map from the Road Atlas © 1994 by Rand McNally; (right) © Encyclopædia Britannica, Inc.; **xii** (bottom right), **xiii** (right) Holly Cooper-Olds; **xviii** (top left, center left, bottom left) Christine McCabe/ ©Encyclopædia Britannica, Inc.; **1** James Alexander; **39** Holly Cooper-Olds; **49** James Alexander

Photographs
x Historic Urban Plans, Inc.; **xiii** Courtesy of Michigan State University Museum.; **xvii** © Corbis; **xviii** Victoria Smith/HRW;**5** M.C. Escher "Symmetry Drawing E21" and "Symmetry Drawing E69" © 2005 The M.C. Escher Company-Holland. All rights reserved. www.mcescher.com; **17** © Age Fotostock/SuperStock; **25** (top) Sam Dudgeon/HRW Photo; (middle) Victoria Smith/HRW; (bottom) EyeWire/ PhotoDisc/Getty Images; **30** PhotoDisc/Getty Images; **32, 40** Victoria Smith/HRW

Contents

Dear Teacher,

Welcome! *Mathematics in Context* is designed to reflect the National Council of Teachers of Mathematics *Principles and Standards for School Mathematics* and the results of decades of classroom-based education research. *Mathematics in Context* was designed according to principles of Realistic Mathematics Education, a Dutch approach to mathematics teaching and learning where mathematical content is grounded in a variety of realistic contexts to promote student engagement and understanding of mathematics. The term *realistic* is meant to convey that the contexts and mathematics can be made "real in your mind." Rather than relying on you to explain and demonstrate generalized definitions, rules, or algorithms, students investigate questions directly related to a particular context and develop mathematical understanding and meaning from that context.

The curriculum encompasses nine units per grade level. *Reallotment* is designed to be the second unit in the Geometry and Measurement strand, but it also lends itself to independent use—to introduce students to methods for measuring perimeter, area, and volume of geometric shapes.

In addition to the Teacher's Guide and Student Books, *Mathematics in Context* offers the following components that will inform and support your teaching:

- *Teacher Implementation Guide,* which provides an overview of the complete system and resources for program implementation.

- *Number Tools* and *Algebra Tools,* which are blackline master resources that serve as review sheets or practice pages to support the development of basic skills and extend student understanding of concepts developed in Number and Algebra units.

- *Mathematics in Context Online,* which is a rich, balanced resource for teachers, students, and parents looking for additional information, activities, tools, and support to further students' mathematical understanding and achievements.

Thank you for choosing *Mathematics in Context.* We wish you success and inspiration!

Sincerely,

The Mathematics in Context Development Team

Reallotment and the NCTM Principles and Standards for School Mathematics for Grades 6–8

The process standards of Problem Solving, Reasoning and Proof, Communication, Connections, and Representation are addressed across all *Mathematics in Context* units.

In addition, this unit specifically addresses the following PSSM content standards and expectations:

Geometry

In grades 6–8, all students should:

- precisely describe, classify, and understand relationships among types of two- and three-dimensional objects;
- understand relationships of the parts of similar objects;
- describe sizes, positions, and orientations of shapes under informal transformations such as flips, turns, slides, and scaling;
- draw geometric objects with specific properties;
- use two-dimensional representations of three-dimensional objects to visualize and solve problems;
- use visual tools to represent and solve problems;
- use geometric models to represent and explain numerical and algebraic relationships; and
- recognize and apply geometric ideas and relationships in areas outside the classroom, such as art, science, and so on.

Measurement

In grades 6–8, all students should:

- understand both metric and customary systems of measurement;
- understand relationships and conversion of units;
- understand, select, and use appropriate units to measure angles, perimeter, area, surface area, and volume;
- use common benchmarks to select appropriate methods for estimating measurements;
- develop and use formulas to determine the circumference of circles and the area of triangles, parallelograms, trapezoids, and circles and develop strategies to find the area of more complex shapes;
- develop strategies to determine the surface area and volume of selected prisms and cylinders;
- select and apply techniques and tools to accurately find length, area, and volume to appropriate levels of precision; and
- solve problems involving scale factors, using ratio and proportion.

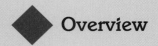

Math in the Unit

This unit assumes that students know and can do the following with understanding:

- perform operations with whole numbers, fractions, and decimal numbers;

- use a calculator when appropriate;

- identify basic geometric shapes, such as a square, rectangle, quadrilateral, triangle, parallelogram, cylinder, and pyramid;

- recognize the difference between area and perimeter;

- work with simple measurement units such as meter (m), centimeter (cm), square centimeter (cm^2), cubic centimeter (cm^3), and so on;

- recognize the difference between metric and customary units of measurement and their basic properties;

- measure lengths both in metric units as well as customary units; and

- use 2-dimensional representations of 3-dimensional objects.

In *Reallotment*, students develop their conceptual understanding of area and volume. This provides the foundation for developing and using a variety of strategies to find areas and volumes. These strategies range from informal methods, such as counting units, to formal methods, such as using formulas. Students develop formal vocabulary related to shapes, area, and volume: they use terminology such as *length, width, base, and height, area, surface area, volume, perimeter, diameter, radius, circumference, square*, and *cubic units*. They also identify geometric figures by name, such as *quadrilaterals, parallelograms*, and *prisms*.

Area

Initially, areas are compared by using intermediate measures such as the number of tulips per field, or the price of pieces of cork. Strategies used for comparing areas, such as counting and reshaping, are introduced. These informal strategies are refined and used to find the area (as the number of units). One of these strategies is the process of reallotment, in which "a part of a figure that is removed is made up for elsewhere."

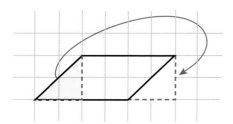

The strategy of realloting becomes a tool students use to find the areas of irregular shapes. Other strategies include:

- using relationships between shapes (for example, the relationship between triangles and rectangles, or between parallelograms and rectangles);

- dividing shapes in smaller parts in which the area is more easily found;

- enclosing shapes in rectangles and subtracting the area of the "extra" parts; and

- using formulas to find the area of rectangles, triangles, parallelograms and circles.

Volume

To find the volume of shapes, several strategies are developed and used as well. Some are similar to the strategies that were developed for finding area:

- counting cubic units ("small blocks"), reshaping, and using formulas;

- dividing solids into smaller parts in which the volume is more easily found;

- enclosing solids in rectangular blocks and subtracting the volume of the "extra" parts; and

- using formulas.

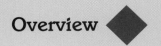

Students use the formulas: *Volume = area of slice × height* and *Volume = area of base × height.* They reason about shapes for which this formula can be applied and when it cannot be applied.

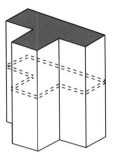

Units

Students use both non-standard units (triangles, tulips, dots, blocks) and standard units to measure and describe area and volume. They use standard units from the metric system (such as square and cubic centimeters) as well as units from the customary system, such as square and cubic inches, yards, and so on. Relationships between different units of measure within each system are explored and applied.

Fractions

Finding the areas of rectangular floors with sides that are partly fractional pre-formally addresses the multiplication of mixed numbers.

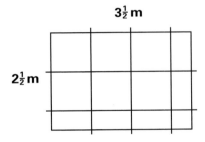

This strategy is later used in other contexts for multiplying fractions, for example, in the context of probability, and is referred to as *the area model.*

Later in the unit, students solve problems that formalize their understanding of the relationships between perimeter and area, and volume and surface area. Students are guided to "reinvent" formulas for the circumference and area of a circle. The concept and value of π is also introduced.

When students have finished this unit they can:

- understand the concepts of area, surface area, and volume;
- use informal and pre-formal strategies involving transformations to estimate and compute the area of irregular shapes as well as the area of rectangles, regular polygons, and other polygons;
- use both non-standard units and standard units to measure and describe area;
- understand and use relations between units of measure within the metric system and within the customary system, and use measurement units and tools appropriately for lengths, areas, and volumes;
- use formal vocabulary and methods for calculating area;
- estimate and calculate the perimeter of shapes and the enlargements of shapes; and
- find the volume of shapes using informal and formal strategies.

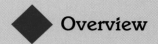
Geometry and Measurement Strand: An Overview

In the MiC units, measurement concepts and skills are not treated as a separate strand. Many measurement topics are closely related to what students learn in geometry. The geometry and measurement units contain topics such as similarity, congruency, perimeter, area, and volume. The identification of and application with a variety of shapes, both two-dimensional and three dimensional, is also addressed.

The developmental principles behind geometry in *Mathematics in Context* are drawn from Hans Freudenthal's idea of "grasping space." Throughout the strand, ideas of geometry and measurement are explored. Geometry includes movement and space—not just the study of shapes. The major goals for this strand are to develop students' ability to describe what is seen from different perspectives and to use principles of orientation and navigation to find their way from one place to another.

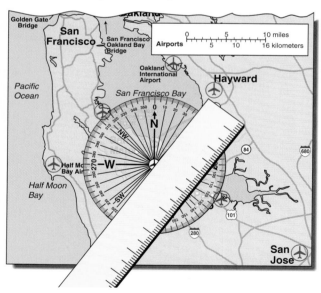

The emphasis on spatial sense is related to how most people actually use geometry. The development of students' spatial sense allows them to solve problems in the real world, such as identifying a car's blind spots, figuring out how much material to buy for a project, deciding whether a roof or ramp is too steep, and finding the height or length of something that cannot be measured directly, such as a tree or a building.

Mathematical content

In *Mathematics in Context*, geometry is firmly anchored in the physical world. The problem contexts involve space and action, and students represent these physical relationships mathematically.

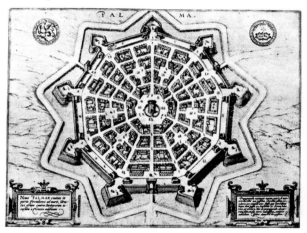

Throughout the curriculum, students discover relationships between shapes and develop the ability to explain and use geometry in the real world. By the end of the curriculum, students work more formally with such geometric concepts as parallelism, congruence, and similarity, and use traditional methods of notation as well.

Pathways through the Geometry and Measurement Strand
(Arrows indicate prerequisite units.)

Level 1

Figuring All the Angles

Reallotment

Level 2

Made to Measure

Packages and Polygons

Triangles and Beyond

Level 3

It's All the Same

Looking at an Angle

Organization of the Geometry and Measurement Strand

Visualization and representation is a pervasive theme in the Geometry strand and is developed in all of the Geometry and Measurement strand units. The units are organized into two substrands: Orientation and Navigation, and Shape and Construction. The development of measurement skills and concepts overlaps these two substrands and is also integrated throughout other *Mathematics in Context* units in Number, Algebra, and Data Analysis.

Orientation and Navigation

The Orientation and Navigation substrand is introduced in *Figuring All the Angles*, in which students are introduced to the cardinal, or compass, directions and deal with the problems that arise when people in different positions describe a location with directions. Students use maps and compass headings to identify the positions of airplanes. They look at angles as turns, or changes in direction, as well as the track made by a sled in the snow. They discern different types of angles and learn formal notations and terms: vertex, $\angle A$, and so on. The rule for the sum of the angles in a triangle is informally introduced. To find angle measurements students use instruments such as a protractor and compass card.

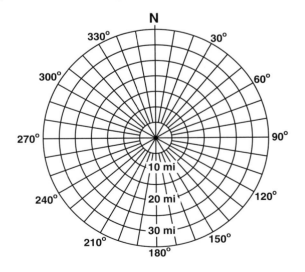

In *Looking at an Angle*, the last unit in the Geometry strand, the tangent ratio is informally introduced. The steepness of a vision line, the sun's rays, a ladder, and the flight path of a hang glider can all be modeled by a right triangle. Considering the glide ratio of hang gliders leads to formalization of the tangent ratio. Two other ratios between the sides of a right triangle are introduced, the sine and the cosine. This leads to formalization of the use of the Pythagorean theorem and its converse.

Shape and Construction

Reallotment is the first unit in the Shape and Construction substrand. Students measure and calculate the perimeters and areas of quadrilaterals, circles, triangles, and irregular polygons. Students learn and use relations between units of measurement within the Customary System and the Metric System.

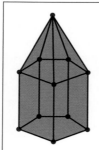

Does Euler's formula work for a five-sided tower? Explain your answer

Solids are introduced in *Packages and Polygons*. Students compare polyhedra with their respective nets, use bar models to understand the concept of rigidity, and use Euler's formula to formally investigate the relationships among the numbers of faces, vertices, and edges of polyhedra.

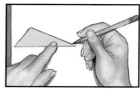
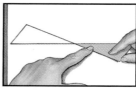
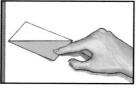

In *Triangles and Beyond*, students develop a more formal understanding of the properties of triangles, which they use to construct triangles. The concepts of parallel lines, congruence, and transformation are introduced, and students investigate the properties of parallel lines and parallelograms. A preformal introduction to the Pythagorean theorem is presented.

After studying this unit, students should be able to recognize and classify triangles and quadrilaterals. In the unit *It's All the Same*, students develop an understanding of congruency, similarity, and the properties of similar triangles and then use these ideas to solve problems. Their work with similarity and parallelism leads them to make generalizations about the angles formed when a transversal intersects parallel lines, and the Pythagorean theorem is formalized.

Measurement

The concept of a measurement system, standardized units, and their application overlaps the substrands of Orientation and Navigation, and Shape and Construction. Furthermore, the development and application of measurement skills is integrated throughout units in the Number, Algebra, and Data Analysis strands, through topics such as use of ratio and proportion, finding and applying scale factors, and solving problems involving rates (for instance, distance-velocity-time relationships).

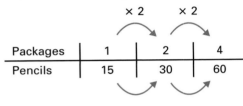

In *Mathematics in Context*, the Metric System is used not only as a measurement system, but also as a model to promote understanding of decimal numbers.

The unit *Made to Measure* is a thematic measurement unit where students work with standard and non-standard units to understand the systems and processes of measurement. They begin by studying historic units of measure such as foot, pace, and fathom (the length of outstretched arms). Students use their own measurements in activities about length, area, volume, and angle and then examine why standardized units are necessary for each.

The relationships between measurement units are embedded in the number unit, *Models You Can Count On*, where students explore conversions between measures of length within the Metric System. The measurement of area in both Metric and Customary Systems is explicitly addressed in the unit *Reallotment*. Students also learn some simple relationships between metric and customary measurement units, such as 1 kilogram is about 2.2 pounds, and other general conversion rules to support estimations across different measurement systems. In *Reallotment*, *Made to Measure*, and *Packages and Polygons*, the concepts of volume and surface area are developed. Strategies that were applied to find area measurements in *Reallotment* are used to derive formulas for finding the volume of a cylinder, pyramid, and cone.

Visualization and Representation

Visualization and representation is a component of every geometry unit. In *Mathematics in Context*, this theme refers to exploring figures from different perspectives and then communicating about their appearance or characteristics.

In *Reallotment*, students use visualizations and representations to find the areas of geometric figures. They decide how to reshape geometric figures and group smaller units into larger, easy-to-count units. They also visualize and represent the results for changing the dimensions of a solid. In the unit *It's All the Same*, students visualize triangles to solve problems.

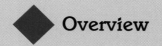
Student Assessment in Mathematics in Context

As recommended by the NCTM *Principles and Standards for School Mathematics* and research on student learning, classroom assessment should be based on evidence drawn from several sources. An assessment plan for a *Mathematics in Context* unit may draw from the following overlapping sources:

- **observation—As students work individually or in groups, watch for evidence of their understanding of the mathematics.**

- **interactive responses—Listen closely to how students respond to your questions and to the responses of other students.**

- **products—Look for clarity and quality of thought in students' solutions to problems completed in class, homework, extensions, projects, quizzes, and tests.**

Assessment Pyramid

When designing a comprehensive assessment program, the assessment tasks used should be distributed across the following three dimensions: mathematics content, levels of reasoning, and difficulty level. The Assessment Pyramid, based on Jan de Lange's theory of assessment, is a model used to suggest how items should be distributed across these three dimensions. Over time, assessment questions should "fill" the pyramid.

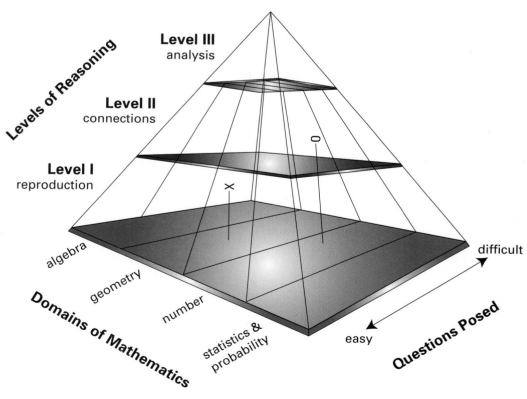

Levels of Reasoning

Level I questions typically address:

- recall of facts and definitions and
- use of technical skills, tools, and standard algorithms.

As shown in the pyramid, Level I questions are not necessarily easy. For example, Level I questions may involve complicated computation problems. In general, Level I questions assess basic knowledge and procedures that may have been emphasized during instruction. The format for this type of question is usually short answer, fill-in, or multiple choice. On a quiz or test, Level I questions closely resemble questions that are regularly found in a given unit, substituted with different numbers and/or contexts.

Level II questions require students to:

- integrate information;
- decide which mathematical models or tools to use for a given situation; and
- solve unfamiliar problems in a context, based on the mathematical content of the unit.

Level II questions are typically written to elicit short or extended responses. Students choose their own strategies, use a variety of mathematical models, and explain how they solved a problem.

Level III questions require students to:

- make their own assumptions to solve open-ended problems;
- analyze, interpret, synthesize, reflect; and
- develop one's own strategies or mathematical models.

Level III questions are always open-ended problems. Often, more than one answer is possible and there is a wide variation in reasoning and explanations. There are limitations to the type of Level III problems that students can be reasonably expected to respond to on time-restricted tests.

The instructional decisions a teacher makes as he or she progresses through a unit may influence the level of reasoning required to solve problems. If a method of problem solving required to solve a Level III problem is repeatedly emphasized during instruction, the level of reasoning required to solve a Level II or III problem may be reduced to recall knowledge, or Level I reasoning. A student who does not master a specific algorithm during a unit but solves a problem correctly using his or her own invented strategy may demonstrate higher-level reasoning than a student who memorizes and applies an algorithm.

The "volume" represented by each level of the Assessment Pyramid serves as a guideline for the distribution of problems and use of score points over the three reasoning levels.

These assessment design principles are used throughout *Mathematics in Context*. The Goals and Assessment charts that highlight ongoing assessment opportunities—on pages xvi and xvii of each Teacher's Guide—are organized according to levels of reasoning.

In the Lesson Notes section of the Teacher's Guide, ongoing assessment opportunities are also shown in the Assessment Pyramid icon located at the bottom of the Notes column.

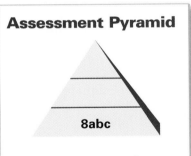

Assessment Pyramid

8abc

Compare the areas of shapes using a variety of strategies and measuring units.

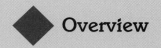
Goals and Assessment

In the *Mathematics in Context* curriculum, unit goals, organized according to levels of reasoning described in the Assessment Pyramid on page xiv, relate to the strand goals and the NCTM *Principles and Standards for School Mathematics.* The *Mathematics in Context* curriculum is designed to help students demonstrate their understanding of mathematics in each of the categories listed below. Ongoing assessment opportunities are also indicated on their respective pages throughout the Teacher's Guide by an Assessment Pyramid icon.

It is important to note that the attainment of goals in one category is not a prerequisite to attaining those in another category. In fact, students should progress simultaneously toward several goals in different categories. The Goals and Assessment table is designed to support preparation of an assessment plan.

	Goal	Ongoing Assessment Opportunities		Unit Assessment Opportunities	
Level I: Conceptual and Procedural Knowledge	**1.** Identify, describe, and classify geometric figures.	**Section A** **Section B**	p. 3, #5a p. 16, #5b	**Quiz 2**	#1c, 4
	2. Compare the length and areas of shapes using a variety of strategies and measuring units.	**Section A** **Section C**	p. 3, #5a p. 27, #5 p. 28, #8abc	**Quiz 1** **Quiz 2**	#1 #1abc
	3. Estimate and compute the areas of geometric figures.	**Section A** **Section B** **Section C** **Section D**	p. 8, #13b, 14 p. 14, #3 p. 16, #8 p. 20, #14 p. 21, #18 p. 31, #14 p. 44, #20a	**Quiz 1** **Quiz 2** **Test**	#2, 3, 4ab #2a, 4 #1ab
	4. Create and work with tessellation patterns.	**Section A**	p. 4, #7b p. 5, #9b	**Test**	#2
	5. Use blocks and visualize geometric models to find surface area and volume.	**Section E**	p. 50, #4 p. 52, #8ab p. 53, #10b p. 54, #14b	**Test**	#4a, 5a

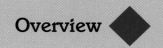

	Goal	Ongoing Assessment Opportunities	Unit Assessment Opportunities
Level II: Reasoning, Communicating, Thinking, and Making Connections	**6.** Understand which units and tools are appropriate to estimate and measure area, perimeter, surface area, and volume.	**Section C** p. 29 #10 **Section E** p. 49, #1ab	**Quiz 1** #3, 4ab **Quiz 2** #1c **Test** #2, 4b
	7. Understand the structure and use of standard systems of measurement, both metric and customary.	**Section C** p. 29, #9 p. 33, #16 **Section D** p. 53, #11, 12	**Quiz 2** #2b
	8. Use the concepts of perimeter and area to solve realistic problems.	**Section D** p. 37, #1 p. 38, #4 p. 45, #21abc	**Quiz 2** #3ab
	9. Use various strategies to find the volume of solids.	**Section E** p. 50, #3 p. 53, #10a p. 57, #19 p. 58, #21abc	**Test** #3

	Goal	Ongoing Assessment Opportunities	Unit Assessment Opportunities
Level III: Modeling, Generalizing, and Non-Routine Problem Solving	**10.** Analyze the effect a systematic change in dimension has on area, perimeter, and volume.	**Section D** p. 38, #5 p. 40, #7, 8 p. 45, #22ab	**Quiz 2** #3b **Test** #3, 5b
	11. Generalize formulas and procedures for determining area and volume.	**Section B** p. 18, #11b p. 19, #13a **Section E** p. 54, #14a	

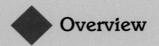

Materials Preparation

The following items are the necessary materials and resources to be used by the teacher and students throughout the unit. For further details, see the Section Overviews and the Materials section at the top of the Hints and Comments column on each teacher page. Note: Some contexts and problems can be enhanced through the use of optional materials. These optional materials are listed in the corresponding Hints and Comments column.

Student Resources

Quantities listed are per student.
- **Letter to the Family**
- **Student Activity Sheets 1–14**

Teacher Resources

No resources required

Student Materials

Quantities listed are per student, unless otherwise indicated.
- **Calculator**
- **Centimeter graph paper (five sheets per student)**
- **Centimeter ruler**
- **Compass (for drawing circles)**
- **Empty tissue boxes (one per group of students)**
- **Graph paper (five sheets per student)**
- **Inch rulers**
- **Index cards (4 in. by 6 in.)**
- **Meter stick (one per group of students)**
- **Scissors**
- **Self-stick notes (two per group of students)**
- **String, between 20 cm and 30 cm long**
- **Tape (one roll per pair or group of students)**

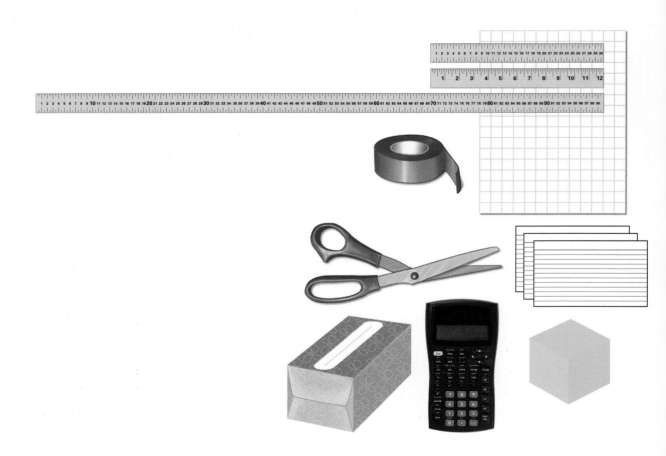

B R I T A N N I C A

Mathematics in Context

Student Material and Teaching Notes

◆ Contents

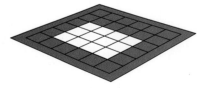

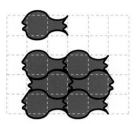

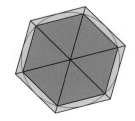

Dear Student,

Welcome to the unit *Reallotment*.

In this unit, you will study different shapes and how to measure certain characteristics of each. You will also study both two- and three-dimensional shapes.

You will figure out things such as how many people can stand in your classroom. How could you find out without packing people in the entire classroom?

You will also investigate the border or perimeter of a shape, the amount of surface or area a shape covers, and the amount of space or volume inside a three-dimensional figure.

How can you make a shape like the one here that will cover a floor, leaving no open spaces?

In the end, you will have learned some important ideas about algebra, geometry, and arithmetic. We hope you enjoy the unit.

Sincerely,

The Mathematics in Context Development Team

Section Focus

The instructional focus of Section A is to:

- **develop an understanding of the concept of area;**
- **compare, estimate, and compute areas of shapes using a variety of strategies and measuring units; and**
- **develop an understanding of the concept of reallotment.**

Pacing and Planning

Day 1: Leave and Trees		Student pages 1 and 2
INTRODUCTION	Problem 1	Compare the area of leaves using informal strategies.
CLASSWORK	Problems 2–4f	Compare the area of irregular and regular shapes.
HOMEWORK	Problems 4g–4j	Compare areas to estimate the price of a piece of cork.

Day 2: Reasonable Prices (Continued)		Student pages 3–7
INTRODUCTION	Problem 5	Compare areas to estimate tile prices.
CLASSWORK	Problems 6–9	Identify the basic design in a tessellation.
HOMEWORK	Problems 10–12	Draw the shape of the state you live in and compare the area of various states.

Day 3: Islands and Shapes		Student pages 8 and 9
INTRODUCTION	Review homework.	Review homework from Day 2.
CLASSWORK	Problems 13 and 14	Estimate area using a square grid.
HOMEWORK	Problem 15	Determine the area of shapes.

Day 4: Summary		Student pages 10–12
INTRODUCTION	Review homework.	Review homework from Day 3.
CLASSWORK	Check Your Work	Student self-assessment: Estimate and find the area of various shapes.
HOMEWORK	For Further Reflection	Describe the process of reallotment.

Additional Resources: Additional Practice, Section A, page 64

Materials

Student Resources

Quantities listed are per student.

- Letter to the Family
- **Student Activity Sheets 1–7**

Teachers Resources

No resources required

Student Materials

Quantities listed are per student

- Graph paper (one sheet)

* See Hints and Comments for optional materials.

Learning Lines

Compare Area

Students use estimation and informally use the concepts of ratio and proportion to compare areas of different-sized shapes. For example, students place one shape on the top of another and look at the overlapping sections. They also use non-conventional units of measure, such as dot patterns, to compare the areas of shapes (they estimate or count the numbers of dots in two shapes). The strategies students use to compare the areas of shapes in this section not only are important in developing their understanding of area and their ability to determine area, but also lay a foundation that will help them better understand how formal area formulas are derived in Section B.

Area

The concept of area—the number of measuring units needed to cover a shape—is implicitly introduced. The mathematical term *area* is not used until after students have experienced filling the interior of a two-dimensional shape.

Tessellations

Tessellations are patterns that fill a plane using congruent copies of a figure that do not overlap. For example, a tessellation can be made by covering a plane using regular triangles. A tessellation pattern can be created by beginning with a basic shape, cutting portions out of one part, and pasting them onto another part. These patterns reinforce the concept of reallotment, a powerful tool for estimating and computing area.

Measuring Units

First, students use a square tile with a given price as a measuring unit to determine the sizes and prices of tiles. The use of the square as a measuring unit is introduced as a mathematical convention and related to the relative cost of different-sized tiles. Then a rectangular grid is used to compare and estimate the areas of shapes. The number of measuring units needed to cover the shape is the area of a shape.

Strategies

The strategies that are used to find the number of square units that cover a shape generally deal with reallotting (or reshaping) a shape. A shape can be seen as the sum of other shapes or as a portion of another shape. A shape can also be rearranged to form a different shape by cutting and pasting. The strategies that students develop in this section are:

- counting the number of whole squares in a shape and estimating the number of squares that the remaining pieces will make;
- subdividing the shape into parts that are easy to work with;
- reshaping the figure by cutting and pasting so that the area of the new shape can be found easily;
- enclosing the shape in a rectangle and subtracting the areas outside the shape; and
- using relationships between shapes.

For example, the area enclosed by a right triangle is exactly one-half of the area enclosed by a rectangle that has sides of the same lengths. This concept can also be used to find the area of other triangles.

At the End of This Section: Learning Outcomes

Students have further developed their understanding of area, developed strategies to compare and estimate areas, and explored strategies for measuring the area of various shapes using squares as a unit for area.

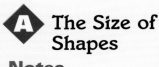 
1 This problem can be introduced by discussing how chocolate leaves would be used on cakes and why a baker would want to know how much chocolate covers a leaf. Cost would be a significant factor if making many leaves.

2 Observe as students work on this problem. Students may want to just guess at the sizes, but encourage them to use a method such as tracing, dividing the space and recombining, or creating a model to make a comparison. The forests are similar on purpose.

The Size of Shapes

Leaves and Trees

Here is an outline of an elm leaf and an oak leaf. A baker uses these shapes to create cake decorations.

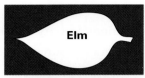

Suppose that one side of each leaf will be frosted with a thin layer of chocolate.

1. Which leaf will have more chocolate? Explain your reasoning.

This map shows two forests separated by a river and a swamp.

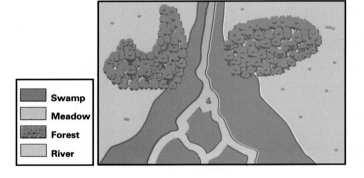

Swamp
Meadow
Forest
River

2. Which forest is larger? Use the figures below and describe the method you used.

Figure A   **Figure B**

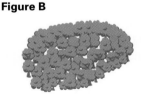

Reaching All Learners

Hands-On Learning

Have students trace or cut out the leaves or forests to compare them. Students could also cut off overlapping pieces to model the reallotment procedure.

Accommodation

An overhead transparency and a copy of the graph paper on a transparency works well to compare these sizes.

Solutions and Samples

1. The oak leaf will have more chocolate frosting, but the leaves are very close in size. Students may trace one leaf and place it over the other leaf to see the non-overlapping areas. Some students may need to cut and paste their tracings.

Students may also use graph paper to count the number of complete squares the leaves cover. They can combine leftover pieces to form new squares and then compare the number of squares each leaf covers.

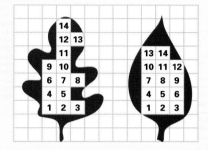

2. Figure B is slightly larger. Students may use the same tracing strategy mentioned for problem 1.

Students may also use graph paper to count the number of complete squares the forests cover. They can combine leftover pieces to form new squares and then compare the number of squares each forest covers.

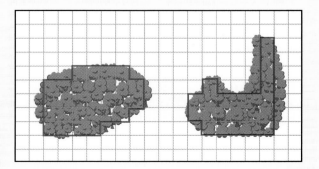

Hints and Comments

Materials

tracing paper, optional (one sheet per pair or group of students);
graph paper, optional (one sheet per pair or group of students);
scissors, optional (one pair per student);
glue or tape, optional (one bottle or roll per pair or group of students)

Overview

Students informally explore the concept of area by developing their own methods to compare the sizes of different shapes. The term *area* is not yet introduced.

About the Mathematics

The context of the problems on this page encourages students to focus on the concept of area and should discourage them from confusing area with perimeter. Several strategies for comparing the areas of different shapes can be used:

- putting one shape on top of the other and then focusing on the overlap;
- cutting and pasting one shape onto another shape to see whether or not it can cover the other shape;
- counting the number of squares on each shape.

These problems show that squares can be used to compare the sizes of shapes. Each square represents a part of the shape. This strategy informally introduces the concept of area: the number of measuring units needed to cover a shape.

Planning

Encourage students to invent their own strategies using any of the materials listed above to compare the areas of the shapes. Students can work in pairs or in small groups on problems 1 and 2. After students finish, review the various methods they used to solve the problems.

Comments About the Solutions

1. and 2. Students' discussions while working in pairs or small groups may motivate them to find more accurate ways to compare the areas of shapes, for example, using graph paper with smaller squares.

◢A The Size of Shapes

Notes

3 Some students will immediately count the tulips across the top row and down the first column and multiply these numbers. Ask these students to convince others that this strategy works.

Reinforce the methods used to compare on page 1.

Using a transparency to compare Fields A and B allows students to see how they are the same size.

4 Students should say how they figured out the prices.

Tulip Fields

Field A **Field B**

Field C

Here are three fields of tulips.

3. Which field has the most tulip plants? Use the tulip fields on **Student Activity Sheet 1** to justify your answer.

Reasonable Prices

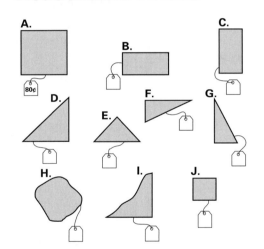

A.

B.

C.

D.

E.

F.

G.

80¢

H.

I.

J.

Mary Ann works at a craft store. One of her duties is to price different pieces of cork. She decides that $0.80 is a reasonable price for the big square piece (figure **A**). She has to decide on the prices of the other pieces.

4. Use **Student Activity Sheet 2** to find the prices of the other pieces. Note: All of the pieces have the same thickness.

Reaching All Learners

Extension

Display student methods for comparing the leaves or forests from page 1. Those methods include making models, tracing, counting, dividing a shape into smaller pieces, and recombining pieces. These methods can be used throughout this section.

Advanced Learners

Ask students to find a piece of cork worth $0.25 or $0.10 or multiple shapes worth one price, such as three different shapes worth $0.40 or $1.20.

Solutions and Samples

3. Field C. It has 296 tulips, while fields A and B each have 242. Students may multiply the number of tulips in one row by the number of tulips in one column.

Field A: 22 × 11 = 242 tulips

Field B: 11 × 22 = 242 tulips

Field C: 8 × 37 = 296 tulips.

Students may also trace and compare fields A and B as illustrated below.

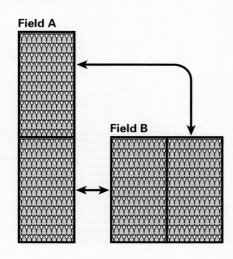

Field A

Field B

4. Estimates will vary. Sample student responses:

b. $0.40

c. $0.40

d. $0.40

e. $0.20

f. $0.20

g. $0.20

h. $0.40

i. $0.40

j. $0.20

Hints and Comments

Materials

Student Activity Sheets 1 and **2** (one per student); scissors, optional (one pair per student); glue or tape, optional (one bottle or roll per pair or group of students); tracing paper, optional (one sheet per student)

Overview

Students compare the areas of three tulip fields and, using a variety of strategies, determine which field has the most tulips. They estimate the prices of pieces of cork of different shapes and sizes by comparing the area of each piece with the area of a square piece of cork priced at 80 cents.

About the Mathematics

Some students may compare the areas of the tulip fields by cutting and rearranging the shape of one field and pasting it onto the shape of another field. This strategy is based on a property of area: when a shape is subdivided, cut, and rearranged, the original area remains intact.

Other students may use the strategy of counting and estimating the total number of tulips in each rectangular field. Some students may count the number of tulips in one row, then add the same number for the second row, and so on (for example, 11, 22, 33, 44, and so on). Other students will use multiplication to find the number of tulips in 22 rows of 11 tulips each. Using these counting strategies will ensure that students will develop a better understanding of the area formula,

$A = l \times w$, which is introduced in Section B.

In problem 4, the concept of comparing areas of different shapes is extended to the concept of comparing prices of different-shaped items based on the area of each item. Students may estimate the areas of the triangular shapes without using a formula by comparing them to the areas of the rectangles and the square. The formula for finding the area of a triangle will be investigated and used in Section D.

Comments About the Solutions

Students should be able to reason about the areas of the different pieces using the fraction concepts they learned in the unit *Fraction Times*. For example, piece J fits four times onto piece A, so it is one-fourth of piece A, and the price will be one-fourth of $0.80 (80 ÷ 4 = 20), or $0.20.

A The Size of Shapes

Notes

Here are drawings of tiles with different shapes. Mary Ann decides a reasonable price for the small tile is $5.

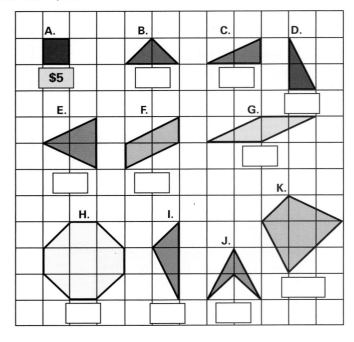

5 In this activity, students must combine, or reallot, pieces to price new tiles in contrast with problem 4 where the large piece was divided into smaller parts to price pieces.

5. a. Use **Student Activity Sheet 3** to find the prices of the other tiles.

b. Reflect Discuss your strategies with some of your classmates. Which tile was most difficult to price? Why?

To figure out prices, you compared the size of the shapes to the $5 square tile. The square was the **measuring unit**. It is helpful to use a measuring unit when comparing sizes.

The number of measuring units needed to cover a shape is called the **area** of the shape.

Assessment Pyramid

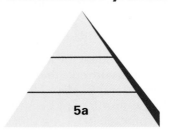

Identify, describe, and classify geometric figures.

Compare the areas of shapes using a variety of strategies and measuring units.

Reaching All Learners

Vocabulary Building

Students may set up a section of their student notebook to record vocabulary that they will encounter throughout this unit. The vocabulary words that are highlighted in blue or boldfaced such as *measuring unit* and *area* can be added to this section and defined with examples or illustrations.

Extension

Have students draw an example of a measuring unit to compare two different shapes. The area of one shape is larger and the area of the other shape is smaller than the measuring unit. Students can display these in the classroom.

Solutions and Samples

5. A. The prices for the other tiles are:

B. $5

C. $5

D. $5

E. $10

F. $10

G. $10

H. $35

I. $7.50

J. $5

K. $22.50

b. The prices can be found by reshaping (transforming the shapes by cutting and pasting and then comparing the shapes with that of the $5 tile). Students may have used the relationships of two shapes to find the area (see About the Mathematics)

Hints and Comments

Materials
Student Activity Sheet 3 (one per student); scissors, optional (one pair per student); glue or tape, optional (one bottle or roll per pair or group of students)

Overview
Students price tiles of different shapes and sizes by comparing their areas to the area of a $5 tile. This problem is similar to problem 4.

About the Mathematics
Students may use several strategies to find the area of a shape.

- Reshape it by cutting and pasting, (see shape B).

- Divide shapes into other shapes, (see shape H).

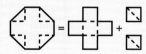

- Take the sum or difference of two other shapes (for example, the difference between shape E and shape B is shape J).

Using these strategies will help students later understand how to devise formulas to find the areas of different regular shapes.

Planning
Students may work on problem 5 in pairs or in small groups. Be sure to discuss the different strategies used so students will begin to develop a repertoire of strategies.

Comments About the Solutions
5. Most students will be able to visually reshape the figures or make drawings to compare the areas of the shapes. Other students may need to cut and paste.

A The Size of Shapes

Notes

7a When you try to tessellate the shapes from problem 5, it is helpful to use a standard number of shapes to "prove" the tessellation. Four of each shape is enough to show that the shapes fit together with no overlaps or gaps.

7b Provide graph paper for this problem.

Tessellations

When you tile a floor, wall, or counter, you want the tiles to fit together without space between them. Patterns without open spaces between the shapes are called **tessellations**.

Sometimes you have to cut tiles to fit together without any gaps. The tiles in the pattern here fit together without any gaps. They form a tessellation.

6. Use the $5 square to estimate the price of each tile.

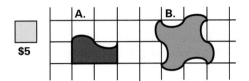

Each of the two tiles in figures **A** and **B** can be used to make a tessellation.

7. **a.** Which of the tiles in problem 5 on page 3 can be used in tessellations? Use **Student Activity Sheet 4** to help you decide.

   b. Choose two of the tiles (from part **a**) and make a tessellation.

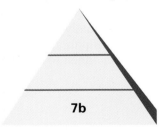
Reaching All Learners

Vocabulary Building

Tessellation is defined on page 4 and students should add it to the vocabulary section of their notebook.

Accommodation

Have students use the computer draw or paint program to create a shape, copy, paste, and try to tessellate it.

Extension

Students could select two or more shapes from problem 5 and create a tessellation, then add details and color. There are video and computer websites that show step-by-step instructions for creating more involved tessellations such as those with rotational or reflectional symmetry. Students can investigate these with parental help and share their findings.

Solutions and Samples

6. a. $10

   b. $20

7. a. All the shapes can be used in tessellations except for shape **h** (the octagon).

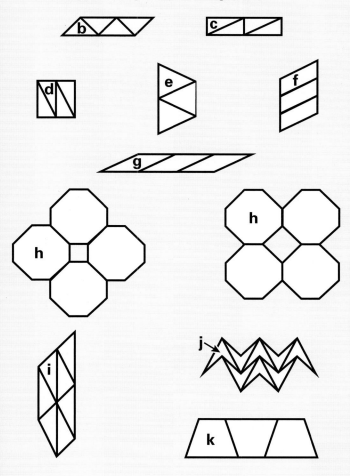

   b. Answers will vary. Make sure that students draw enough of each pattern to show that it is a tessellation.

Hints and Comments

Materials

Student Activity Sheet 4 (one per student); graph paper, optional (one sheet per student); tracing paper, optional (one sheet per student); transparency, optional (one per class); scissors, optional (one pair per student); compass, optional (one per student)

Overview

Students estimate the prices of two tiles that can be used for a tessellation. They then investigate which of the tiles on Student Book page 3 can be used for a tessellation.

About the Mathematics

Students are introduced to tessellations—congruent copies of a figure that do not overlap and have no open spaces. These patterns help students become aware of the concept of reallotment—a powerful tool for estimating area.

Tessellations develop students' understanding of the concepts of area and measuring units, which do not have to be squares. For example, using triangle C on Student Book page 3 as a measuring unit, the area of the rectangle below is four triangles.

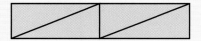

Planning

Students may work in pairs or in small groups on problems 6 and 7. You may ask some students to draw their tessellations for problem 7 on a transparency and show them to the class.

Comments About the Solutions

7. The grid provided on **Student Activity Sheet 4** has a different-sized square unit than that used on pages 3 and 4 of the Student Book. This will prevent students from simply copying or tracing the shape.

Students may have difficulty with the arrow (tile J) and the octagon (tile H). You may suggest that they draw about four of each of these shapes on a piece of graph paper and cut them out. Then students can investigate how the shapes will fit together.

Discuss whether a tessellation can be made of more than one shape. (See, for example, tessellation H: squares can fill up the area in between.)

A The Size of Shapes

Notes

Resources are available to show basic tessellations (patterns in floors) to make designs. Sharing these visuals helps to build spatial awareness and visualization skills. (Escher's work can be found on posters, clothing, cups, desk items, and in books.)

Tessellations often produce beautiful patterns. Artists from many cultures have used tessellations in their work. The pictures below are creations from the Dutch artist M. C. Escher.

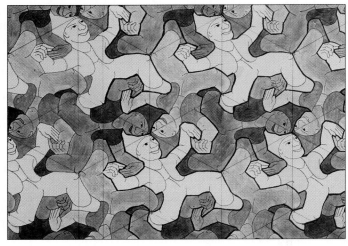

Assessment Pyramid

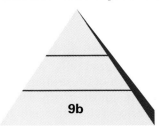

9b

Create and work with tessellation patterns.

Reaching All Learner

Intervention

Cut out shapes that students move around and create a tessellation that shows positive and negative space. Also, graph paper can help students with alignment.

Advanced Learners

Have students investigate the life and work of M.C. Escher and report to the class.

Hints and Comments

Extension

You may have students explore the basic designs for tessellations and discuss their ideas. Some students may include a black-and-white pair of figures as the repeated design in each pattern. You may ask whether they would change their designs if they were to pay attention only to the shape of the repeating design and not its color. Exploring tessellations emphasizes that measuring units for area may include shapes other than squares.

Interdisciplinary Connection

Have students find information on the works of the Dutch artist Maurits Cornelius Escher or on the tessellations found in tile patterns of early Greek or Roman architecture. Ask students to write brief reports about their findings. Some reports might be shared with the class.

Did You Know?

M.C. Escher (1898–1972) was a Dutch graphic artist known for using realistic details to achieve strange visual effects in prints. He was a master of illusion—transforming and distorting images using mathematical tricks. His pictures were of equal interest to mathematicians, psychologists, and the general public and were widely reproduced in the mid-20th century.

A The Size of Shapes

Notes

Post the basic rule for creating tessellations in the classroom: *What is changed in one place must be made up for elsewhere.* Discuss what this means.

8 Students may try to tessellate shapes C and D on graph paper.

9 Provide graph paper to draw and make changes.

Here is one way to make a tessellation. Start with a rectangular tile and change the shape according to the following rule.

What is changed in one place must be made up for elsewhere.

For example, if you add a shape onto the tile like this,

you have to take away the same shape someplace else. Here are a few possibilities.

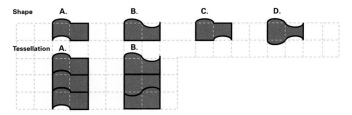

8. How many complete squares make up each of the shapes **A** through **D**?

Shape **D** can be changed into a fish by taking away and adding some more parts. Here is the fish.

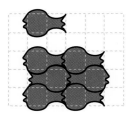

9. a. Draw the shape of the fish in your notebook.

   b. Show in your drawing how you can change the fish back into a shape that uses only whole squares.

   c. How many squares make up one fish?

Another way to ask this last question in part **c** is, "What is the area of one fish measured in squares?" The square is the measuring unit.

Reaching All Learners

Hands-On Activity

Have students create a tessellation using one or more of the shapes on pages 3 or 6. They could figure out how much their individual shape would take up in area and its cost based on a particular cost per square.

Solutions and Samples

8. Each figure **A** through **D** is made up of two whole squares because the shape that is added is taken away someplace else.

9. a. and **b.**

Students can use arrows to show that the parts attached to the head of the fish fit in the body, and the parts that make up the mouth fit in the tail fin. Then the rectangle is back.

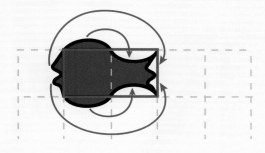

c. 2 squares (see answer to part **b.**)

Hints and Comments

Materials

graph paper (one sheet per student);
colored pencils, optional (one box per student)

Overview

Students learn how to make a new tessellation design by cutting, pasting, and rearranging parts of existing rectangular tiles: reallotment. They further develop their understanding of area and measuring units.

About the Mathematics

When a rectangular tile used as a basic tessellating unit is altered by subtracting a portion from one place and adding it to another, the area remains the same.

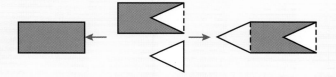

Planning

Students may work in pairs or in small groups on problems 8 and 9.

Extension

You may have students use graph paper and shape **C** (or design a shape by themselves, using cut-and-paste) to create a tessellation. They may use colored pencils to decorate their designs. Escher drawings, as well as students' designs, might make an attractive display in the classroom.

Sample tessellations:

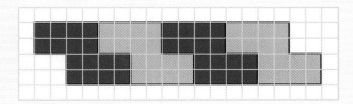

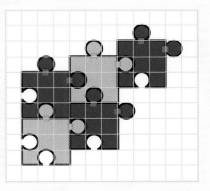

A The Size of Shapes

Notes

10a Relate your state or other states to polygon names. (Examples: Utah is a hexagon. Nevada is a trapezoid. South Dakota is a rectangle.)

11 Refer students to the strategies used on the problems for all previous pages to make their estimates.

Big States, Small States

The shape of a state can often be found on tourism brochures, government stationery, and signs at state borders.

10. a. Without looking at a map, draw the shape of the state in which you live.

b. If you were to list the 50 states from the largest to the smallest in land size, about where would you rank your state?

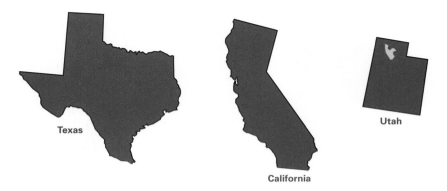

Texas

California

Utah

Three U.S. states, drawn to the same scale, are above.

11. Estimate the answer to the following questions. Explain how you found each estimate.

a. How many Utahs fit into California?

b. How many Utahs fit into Texas?

c. How many Californias fit into Texas?

d. Compare the areas of these three states.

Forty-eight of the United States are **contiguous**, or physically connected. You will find the drawing of the contiguous states on **Student Activity Sheet 5**.

12. Choose three of the 48 contiguous states and compare the area of your state to the area of each of these three states.

Reaching All Learners

Accommodation

A U.S. map puzzle with individual state pieces could be used to compare sizes. Reinforce "reallotment" to compare states.

Extension

Have students use information from almanacs or other resource material to compare the area ranking of the state in which they live to its population ranking. Ask before they see the ranking lists, *Do you think the order of states ranked according to size will be the same order of states when ranked by population? Why or why not?* (No, because population ranking has no relation to the area ranking.)

Solutions and Samples

10. a. Drawings will vary.

b. Answers will vary.

11. a. About two Utahs would fit into California. Accept a range from $1\frac{1}{2}$ to $2\frac{1}{2}$. Explanations will vary. Some students may actually trace and cut out the area of Utah and lay it on California as shown below.

b. About three Utahs would fit into Texas. Accept a range from $1\frac{1}{2}$ to $3\frac{1}{2}$. Explanations will vary. Some students may trace and cut as shown below.

c. Almost two Californias would fit into Texas. Accept a range from $1\frac{1}{2}$ to $2\frac{1}{2}$. Explanations will vary. Some students may trace and cut as shown below.

d. The order from small to large is:

Utah, California (two Utahs), Texas (three Utahs)

12. Answer will vary according to the state in which students reside and the three states they select.

Hints and Comments

Materials
Student Activity Sheet 5 (one per student); almanacs, optional (one per pair or group of students); tracing paper, optional (one sheet per student); graph paper, optional (one sheet per student); scissors, optional (one pair per student)

Overview

Students compare the areas of three states and then draw the shape of their own state using the same scale. Students use a U.S. map to compare the area of their state to the areas of three other states.

About the Mathematics

Problems 10–12 are powerful illustrations of what is meant by the term *area*: the number of measuring units needed to cover an entire region.

Planning

Students may work on problems 10–12 in pairs or in small groups. After students finish problem 11, discuss their solutions and strategies for problems 10b and 11. You may want to orient students to the U.S. map. Be sure they understand the expression *contiguous states*. Discuss students' strategies for problem 12.

Comments About the Solutions

11. Encourage students to devise their own strategies. For parts **a** and **b**, some students may try to cover the other states with as many Utahs as possible. Others may use graph paper to estimate the area of each state and then make relative comparisons.

c. Some students may estimate the areas of both states, while others may use their answers to parts **a** and **b**.

12. Avoid standard units at this stage unless initiated by students. A useful extension of this problem would be to make an inventory of all students' responses in class and ask the students to draw conclusions about the area ranking of all the states that were used.

A The Size of Shapes

Notes

The common units used for area are always squares, because squares and parts of squares can be used to fill a space, and squares fit together without leaving any space in between. The side length of common square units can be inches, centimeters, or any other length unit.

13b Reinforce that estimates aren't exact, but must be reasonable.

14 Students will see that the triangle is half of the square or rectangle in this activity. Be sure to reinforce this idea well. You are building a concrete understanding of why a triangle's area is half that of the rectangle with the same base and height without using a formula.

Islands and Shapes

If a shape is drawn on a grid, you can use the squares of the grid to find the area of the shape. Here are two islands: Space Island and Fish Island.

Space Island   **Fish Island**

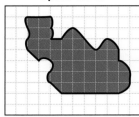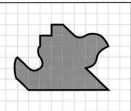

13. **a.** Which island is bigger? How do you know? Use **Student Activity Sheet 6** to justify your answers.

    b. Estimate the area of each island in square units.

Since the islands have an irregular form, you can only estimate the area for these islands.

You can find the exact area for the number of whole squares, but you have to estimate for the remaining parts. Finding the exact area of a shape is possible if the shape has a more regular form.

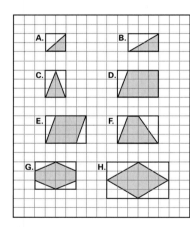

14. What is the area of each of the shaded pieces? Use **Student Activity Sheet 7** to help you. Give your answers in square units. Be prepared to explain your reasoning.

Assessment Pyramid

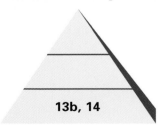

13b, 14

Estimate and compute the areas of geometric figures.

Reaching All Learners

Extension

Have students explain to the class or a small group how they found the areas. Use a transparency for **Student Activity Sheet 7**. Allow students to share various solutions and discuss how the shapes are related.

Intervention

For those students who had difficulties, you may want to use the following problems as extra practice. Or you could use these problems for all students to practice the "enclosing" strategy. (Answers: 4 square units and 14 square units.)

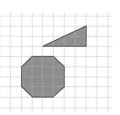

Solutions and Samples

13. a. Space Island is bigger than Fish Island. Explanations will depend on the strategies students used. Sample student response:

For each island, I counted the number of complete squares covered. Then I combined the leftover parts of squares to make complete squares and counted them.

b. Estimates will vary. For Space Island, accept estimates in the range of 35 to 41 square units. For Fish Island, accept estimates in the range of 28 to 34 square units.

14. A. 2 square units

   B. 3 square units

   C. 3 square units

   D. $10\frac{1}{2}$ square units

   E. 9 square units

   F. $7\frac{1}{2}$ square units

   G. 8 square units

   H. 12 square units

Explanations will depend on the strategies students used. Students' reasoning should show the methods used to reallot each figure to find its area.

Hints and Comments

Materials

Student Activity Sheets 6 and **7** (one of each per student);
transparencies of **Student Activity Sheets 6** and **7**, optional (one per class)

Overview

Students compare the areas of two islands and use different strategies to decide which island is the largest. Students determine the areas of different geometric figures.

About the Mathematics

On this page, students start to determine area using one square in the grid as a measuring unit. To find the number of squares that cover a shape, a variety of strategies can be used:

- counting the number of whole squares in a shape and estimating the number of squares that the remaining pieces will make;

- subdividing the shape into parts that are easy to work with;

- reshaping the figure by cutting and pasting so that the area of the new shape can be found easily;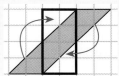

- enclosing the shape in a rectangle and subtracting the areas outside the shape.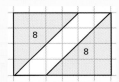

Comments About the Problems

13. Encourage students to estimate the areas of the islands using the grid squares. If students are having difficulty estimating the areas, make a transparency of **Student Activity Sheet 6** to show students' different counting strategies.

14. Finding the areas of figures **A** and **B** can involve the strategy of halving the area of a rectangle. Some students may devise and use a subtraction strategy for figures **E**, **G**, and **H**. Make sure that students include units (squares or square units are acceptable).

A The Size of Shapes

Notes

Try to move students away from reallotting pieces to find the areas.

When you know the area of one shape, you can sometimes use that information to help you find the area of another shape. This only works if you can use some relationship between the two shapes.

Here are some shapes that are shaded.

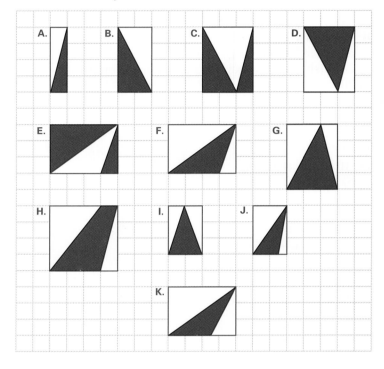

15a Use a transparency to show relationships.

To find relationships, students:

- can focus on the two colors in one shape, complements of each other with respect to the enclosing rectangle;

- may compare shapes and see if one shape is a combination of one or more other shapes, or a part of it.

15. **a.** Choose four blue shapes and describe how you can find the area of each. If possible, use relationships between shapes.

 b. Now find the area (in square units) of each of the blue pieces.

 c. Describe the relationship between the blue area in shapes **C** and **D**.

Reaching All Learners

Accommodation

Make copies of this page for those students who want to draw the grid lines inside the shapes. This will help them to determine the areas.

Solutions and Samples

15. a. Answers will vary since students can choose any four shapes they want. Below are some examples of relationships between shapes students may see:

Shapes **C** and **D** are the complement of each other with respect to the enclosing rectangle; same for **E** and **F**.

Shapes **A** and **B** are half of the enclosing rectangles; this is also true for **I**, although it may be more difficult to recognize.

b. A. 2 square units

B. 4 square units

C. 6 square units

D. 6 square units

E. $7\frac{1}{2}$ square units

F. $4\frac{1}{2}$ square units

G. 6 square units

H. 8 square units

I. 3 square units

J. $2\frac{1}{4}$ square units

K. $3\frac{3}{4}$ square units

c. Sample responses:

- The blue area in shapes **C** and **D** together make the rectangle.
- 12– **C** = **D**, and 12 – **D** = **C**.

Hints and Comments

Materials

transparency of page 15 of the Student Book, optional (one per class)

Overview

Students calculate the areas of triangles.

About the Mathematics

This activity leads students closer to discovering a method or formula to find the area of a triangle. The formula itself should not be introduced at this point. It is important, however, that students see that the area of a right triangle is exactly one-half of the area of a rectangle that has sides of the same lengths, such as in figures **A** and **B**. This concept can also be used to find the area of other triangles, as show below.

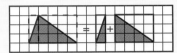

By subtracting the unshaded areas from the total area of the rectangle, the area of the shaded triangle is found. This strategy is especially useful for finding the areas of triangles like figure **F**. Note that the statement "the area of a triangle is one-half of the area of a rectangle" is not always valid. The triangle and rectangle in figure **K** illustrate this.

Planning

Students may work on problem 15 in pairs or in small groups. During the next class session, have students share their strategies with the class.

Comments About the Problems

15. If students simply count the squares in the triangles, encourage them to use a strategy such as halving or subtracting unshaded portions. Some students may see that the area of figure C can be used to find the area of figure D, because they are opposites, or inverse of each other.

The Size of Shapes

Notes

After reading the Summary aloud, you may have students go back through the section to find problems that support the strategies for finding the areas of various shapes. This will make students use the Summary actively as a study tool.

Produce a visual representation of each of the four strategies shown on pages 10 and 11 for measuring the areas of various shapes:

- reallotment;
- relationships;
- divide up; or
- enclose and subtract empty areas.

Summary

This section is about areas (sizes) of shapes. You used different methods to compare the areas of two forests, tulip fields, pieces of cork, tiles, and various states and islands. You:

- may have counted tulips;
- compared different-shaped pieces of cork to a larger square piece of cork; and
- divided shapes and put shapes together to make new shapes.

You also actually found the area of shapes by measuring. Area is described by using square units.

You explored several strategies for measuring the areas of various shapes.

- You counted the number of complete squares inside a shape, then reallotted the remaining pieces to make new squares.

  Inside this shape there are four complete squares.

  The pieces that remain can be combined into four new squares.

 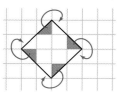

- You may have used relationships between shapes.

  You can see that the shaded piece is half of the rectangle.

  Or you can see that two shapes together make a third one.

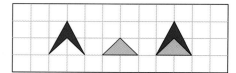

Reaching All Learners

Parent Involvement

Have students discuss the Summary with their parents. Parents often wish to help their child and both may benefit from reviewing the ideas together.

Hints and Comments

Overview

Students read the Summary, which reviews the methods students may have used to compare and find area in this section.

The Size of Shapes

Notes

Students may use the two strategies on this page of the Summary to find the areas of the trapezoid and triangle, then share aloud.

- You may have divided a shape into smaller parts whose area you can find more easily.

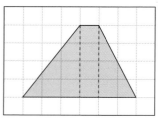

- You may also have enclosed a shape with a rectangle and subtracted the empty areas.

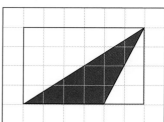

Check Your Work

1. Sue paid $3.60 for a 9 inch (in.)-by-13 in. rectangular piece of board. She cuts the board into three pieces as shown. What is a fair price for each piece?

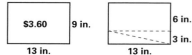

$3.60   9 in.   6 in.   3 in.   13 in.   13 in.

Assessment Pyramid

1

Assesses Section A Goals

Reaching All Learners

Accommodation

Provide a model with three cut pieces. Students can manipulate the shapes to solve this problem. Relate the pieces to fractional parts of the whole. The large piece is $\frac{2}{3}$ of the whole. The smaller pieces are each $\frac{1}{6}$ of the whole or are $\frac{1}{3}$ when combined. Be sure the individual prices add to $3.60.

Intervention

Divide the shape into three equal parts (divide horizontally). Then ask students to price these three equal parts and then figure out the prices of the original pieces. A model with the three original pieces cut would be beneficial, too.

Solutions and Samples

Answers to Check Your Work

1. The biggest rectangular piece of board will cost $2.40, and the two triangular pieces of board will cost $0.60 each.

Sample answer:

The two triangles at the bottom form a 3 x 13 in. piece. I divided the 6 x 13 in. piece in half. Now I have three 3 x 13 in. pieces. Since the whole piece of board costs $3.60, each 3 x 13 in. piece will cost $1.20. So two of the 3 x 13 in. pieces will cost $2.40. A triangular piece is half of a 3 x 13 in. piece, so it costs $0.60.

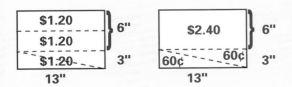

Hints and Comments

Overview

Students finish reading the Summary. Then they use the Check Your Work problems as self-assessment. The answers to these problems are also provided in the Student Book.

2b Remind students that an estimate must be reasonable and that an area label is *always* given in square units. Discuss why this is necessary.

2. Below you see the shapes of two lakes.

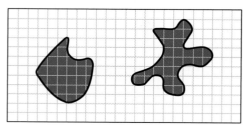

    a. Which lake is bigger? How do you know?

    b. Estimate the area of each lake.

3. Find the area in square units of each of these orange pieces.

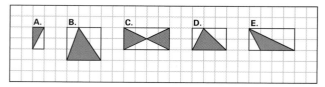

4. Choose two of these shapes and find the area of the green triangles. Explain how you found each area.

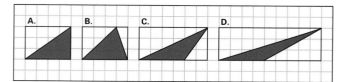

 For Further Reflection

Why do you think this unit is called *Reallotment*?

For Further Reflection

Reflective problems are meant to summarize and discuss important concepts.

Assessment Pyramid

FFR

2ab, 3, 4

Assesses Section A Goals

Reaching All Learners

Extension

Have students explain aloud or draw how to find the areas in problem 3. Can students see the relationship among the triangles in problem 4? They all have the same area. Challenge students to use "Reallotment" to prove that all of the triangles have the same area.

Solutions and Samples

2. a. You might think they are about the same size because if you reshape the right lake into a more compact form, it will be about the same shape and size as the left one. You might also count the number of whole squares in each lake and decide that the lake on the left will be larger because it has more squares.

b. You can use different ways to find your answer. One way is to try to make as many whole squares as you can. The left lake is about 23 squares, and the right lake about 26 squares.

3. A. 1 square unit

B. $4\frac{1}{2}$ square units

C. 4 square units

D. 3 square units

E. 3 square units

4. The area enclosed by each triangle is 6 square units. You can find your answer by:

- reallotting portions of the triangle and
- subtracting unwanted pieces.
  For example, to find the area enclosed by triangle **D**, you may use this subtraction strategy as shown below.

Area enclosed by rectangle:
$3 \times 9 = 27$ square units

Area of unwanted sections:
$7\frac{1}{2} + 13\frac{1}{2} = 21$ square units

Area of shaded region $= 27 - 21 = 6$ square units

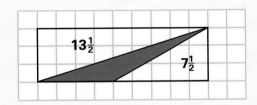

For Further Reflection

Answers will vary.

Student responses should mention the process of moving parts of shapes to either make new shapes or find how much area is covered. They may even mention that they now understand what reallotment means!

Hints and Comments

Overview

Students continue to use the Check Your Work problems as self-assessment. The answers to these problems are also provided on Student Book pages 70 and 71.

Planning

After students complete Section A, you may assign as homework appropriate activities from the Additional Practice section located on Student Book page 64.

Section Focus

The instructional focus of Section B is to:

- further develop students' understanding of the concept of area;
- compare, estimate, and compute areas of shapes using a variety of strategies, such as using squares as measuring units; and
- develop students' formal vocabulary related to shapes and area, using words like *base*, *height*, *area*, and *square unit*, and names such as *quadrilateral* and *parallelogram*.

Pacing and Planning

Day 5: Rectangles		Student pages 13–16
INTRODUCTION	Problems 1 and 2	Find the area enclosed by rectangles.
CLASSWORK	Problems 3 and 4	Determine the prices of different-sized pieces of felt.
ACTIVITY	Activity, page 15	Transform a rectangle into different parallelograms by cutting and pasting.
HOMEWORK	Problems 5 and 6	Use the cutting and pasting strategy to transform parallelograms into a rectangle.

Day 6: Quadrilateral Patterns (Continued)		Student pages 16–18
INTRODUCTION	Problem 7	Find a method to determine the areas enclosed by parallelograms.
CLASSWORK	Problems 8–10	Explain how the prices for different stacks of wood were determined and estimate the price of a slanted stack of wood.
HOMEWORK	Problems 11 and 12a	Find the areas of quadrilaterals enclosed by rectangles and develop a rule.

Day 7: Strategies and Formulas (Continued)		Student pages 19–24
INTRODUCTION	Review homework. Problems 12b and 12c	Review homework from Day 6, and draw two triangles with the same area.
CLASSWORK	Problems 13–18	Apply the formulas for area and find the area of a triangle for which the formula cannot easily be used.
HOMEWORK	Check Your Work	Student self-assessment: Use various strategies to find areas of quadrilaterals and triangles.

Day 8. Summary		
INTRODUCTION	Review homework.	Review homework from Day 7.
ASSESSMENT	Quiz 1	Assessment of Sections A and B Goals
HOMEWORK	For Further Reflection	Compare strategies for finding the area of shapes.

Additional Resources: Additional Practice, Section B, Student Book page 65

Materials

Student Resources

Quantities listed are per student.

- **Student Activity Sheet 8 and 9**

Teachers Resources

No resources required

Student Materials

Quantities listed are per student, unless otherwise noted.

- $4'' \times 6''$ index cards or additional sheet of graph paper
- Graph paper (five sheets)
- Rulers
- Scissors
- Tape (one roll per pair or group of students)

* See Hints and Comments for optional materials.

Learning Lines

Strategies

The strategies for estimating and calculating area that students developed in Section A are made more explicit in this section:

- counting the number of whole squares in a shape and combining the remaining pieces into whole squares;
- reshaping the figure by cutting and pasting so that the area of the new shape can be found easily;
- enclosing the shape in a rectangle and subtracting the areas outside the shape;
- using relationships between shapes; and
- using formulas.

Formulas: Area

The use of base and height measurements leads to formulas for the areas of rectangles, parallelograms, and triangles. Counting strategies for finding area, such as the number of squares in one row, times the number of rows, are an 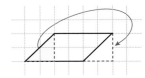 important base to develop students' understanding of the formula: $A_{rectangle} = base \times height$.

To derive a formula for the area of a parallelogram from the area of a rectangle, several strategies can be used, such as the compensating strategy or shifting. The compensating strategy means to cut and paste triangular sections of the parallelogram to reshape the figure into a rectangle.
A diagonal of a parallelogram divides the parallelogram into two congruent triangles. Therefore every triangle can be considered as half of a parallelogram: $A_{triangle} = \frac{1}{2} of base \times height$

At the End of This Section: Learning Outcomes

Students are able to use informal and pre-formal strategies that involve transformations to estimate and compute the area of irregular shapes as well as the area of rectangles and other polygons. Students have further developed formal vocabulary and methods for calculating area. They start to use formulas for finding the area enclosed by rectangles, triangles, and parallelograms.

 **B**

Area Patterns

Rectangles

1. Find the area enclosed by each of the rectangles outlined in the figures below. Explain your methods.

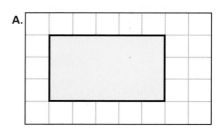

A.

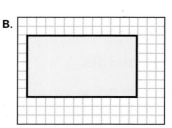

B.

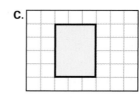

C.

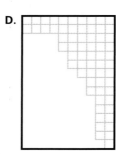

D.

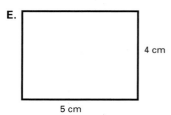

E.

4 cm

5 cm

2a Combine all methods on a chart and post it in the room.

2. **a.** Describe at least two different methods you can use to find the area enclosed by a rectangle.

b. Reflect Which method do you prefer? Why?

Reaching All Learners

Accommodation

Have copies of this page for students who may need to extend or draw in grid lines.

Solutions and Samples

1. A. 15 square units, found by counting or calculating 3 × 5, three rows of 5 squares, or five rows of three squares, 5 × 3

B. 84 square units. Students may have counted, but this is a lot of work; it is easier to count one row or column and multiply with the number of rows or columns. Some students may know and use the rule *length × width*, which is 7 × 12, or 12 × 7.

C. 12 square units. For methods, see **A** and **B**. Students may draw in the "squares."

D. 150 (10 × 15) square units. Students may want to fill in the squares, which is a low-level strategy and must be discouraged here. For other methods, see **B**.

E. 20 square centimeters. Students may draw in squares or use the rule *length × width*.

2. a. Answers will vary. See answers to problem 1.

b. Answers will vary. Make sure students give a reason for their choice.

Hints and Comments

Overview

Students find the area enclosed by rectangles and explain the methods they used.

About the Mathematics

Area is a measure of the space that a two-dimensional figure encloses. Mathematical shapes do not actually have an area; for example, a rectangle is only the outline—it encloses an area. Real things, like a board and glass, have area.

Planning

You may have students work on problems 1 and 2 in pairs or in small groups so that they can share their ideas. Discuss students' methods in class.

Comments About the Solutions

1. Make sure that students include units: squares or square units and square centimeters for figure E. The unit square centimeter and its notation (cm^2) are investigated and made explicit in Section C.

2. The different methods that students may have used are:

   • count all the squares inside the rectangle;

   • count the number of squares in one row or column and then multiply by the number of rows or columns;

   • find the total number of squares by multiplying the number of squares that fit in the length by the number that fit in the width; or

   • use the rule *length × width*.

B Area Patterns

Notes

Discuss what the numbers around the outside of the rectangles mean.

Find the area of the felt measuring unit and note the relationship between the area and the cost numbers.

3 Inform students that rectangle D should have been drawn the same size as the others. It is correctly drawn on **Student Activity Sheet 8**.

Students can share aloud how they found the felt costs on a transparency of **Student Activity Sheet 8**.

Have students notice relationships between figures such as A and C or B and E. Encourage them to use what they know to figure out what they do not know.

Ms. Petry's class wants to make a wall hanging of geometric shapes. They will use different colors of felt for the geometric shapes. The felt is sold in sheets, 4 feet (ft) by 6 ft. Each sheet costs $12. The store will only charge Ms. Petry's class for the shapes that are cut out.

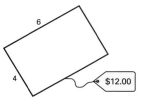

Meggie wants to buy this shaded piece.

3 a. Explain why the piece Meggie wants to buy will cost $6.00.

b. Here are the other shapes they plan to purchase. Use **Student Activity Sheet 8** to calculate the price of the geometric shapes (the shaded pieces).

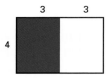

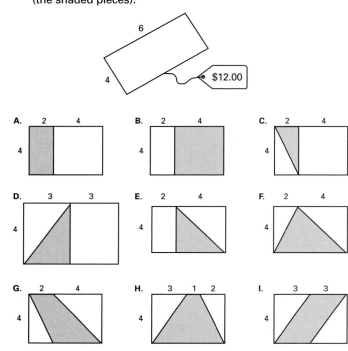

Assessment Pyramid

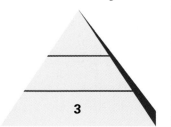

3

Compute the areas of geometric figures.

Reaching All Learners

Accommodation

Provide graph paper or cut-out shapes that students can manipulate and price.

Advanced Learners

Show a piece that would cost $9, $10, or $11, and explain aloud. Show some pieces that would cost only $1. Students can try to find as many pieces as they can that would cost a particular price. Decide what size the smallest piece that was reasonable to sell would be.

Solutions and Samples

3. a. Sample explanation:

Maggie wants to buy half of the piece of felt, so this will cost half of $12, which is $6.

b. A. $4 (third of $12)

B. $8 (two-thirds of $12, or the part that is left over from **A**, which costs $12 − $4)

C. $2 (half of the price of shape **A**)

D. $3 (half of the price of problem 3a)

E. $4 (half of the price of shape **B**)

F. $6 (the price of shape **C** plus the price of shape **E**, or half of the price of shape A plus half of the price of shape **B**)

G. $6 (the price of shape **C** plus the price of shape **E**)

H. $7. Sample strategy:

Divide the large rectangle into three smaller rectangles (one 3 × 4, one 1 × 4, and one 2 × 4), as shown below.

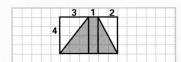

Calculate the cost of the shaded area of each rectangle. The center rectangle is completely shaded, so its area is $\frac{1}{6}$ of a whole sheet. So its cost is $2.

The shaded area of the rectangle on the left is the same as shape **D**. Its cost is $3. (Or the shaded area of the rectangle on the left is half of its total area of 12 square units, which is 6 square units.)

The shaded area of the rectangle on the right is the same as shape **C**. Its cost is $2. (Or the shaded area of the rectangle on the right is also half of its total area of 8 square units, which is 4 square units.)

I. $6 (twice the price of shape **D**)

Hints and Comments

Materials

Student Activity Sheet 8 (one per student)

Overview

Students determine the prices of different-sized pieces of felt using the dimensions and price of one piece.

About the Mathematics

To find the area of the shaded pieces, students may use one of the following strategies: halving; subtraction; constructing a grid; relating one problem to another; or dividing each diagram into a series of smaller rectangles and triangles, calculating the areas of these smaller shapes and sometimes adding areas to equal the shaded area.

Planning

Students can work individually or in pairs on problem 3. Discuss the different methods that are used. This may help students to develop a strategy for finding the area of a triangle.

Comments About the Solutions

3. Students may compare area and use the prices of shapes they have already calculated or can calculate easily, or they may use the relationship between one square and its price of half a dollar (students should not be encouraged to use this method).

Notes

List all the quadrilaterals that students know and draw examples of each polygon by the respective name.

Activity

You may find that tape is easier to use than paste if using an index card to do the activity.

Have the rectangle transformation steps available for students to see and recreate. Some students have difficulty moving the cut-off piece to the right position. Turn around as you demonstrate the cut, move, and paste steps so your example is traveling in the same direction as the students. Some students will grasp this quickly and then can assist others.

Quadrilateral Patterns

A **quadrilateral** is a four-sided figure.

A **parallelogram** is a special type of quadrilateral.

A parallelogram is a four-sided figure with opposite sides parallel.

    4. Is a **rectangle** a parallelogram? Why or why not?

► Activity

Looking for Patterns

You can transform a rectangle into many different parallelograms by cutting and pasting a number of times. Try this on graph paper or use a 4 in.-by-6 in. index card.

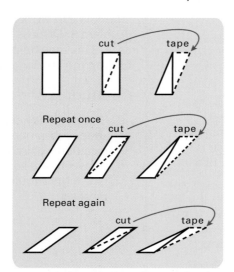

  i. Draw a rectangle that is two units wide and three units high or use the index card as the rectangle.

  ii. Cut along a **diagonal** and then tape to create a new parallelogram.

  iii. Repeat step ii a few more times.

How is the final parallelogram different from the rectangle? How is it the same?

Reaching All Learners

Vocabulary Building

Have students add the words *quadrilateral*, *parallelogram*, and *rectangle* to their notebook vocabulary section along with definitions and illustrations.

Intervention

For the Activity, provide a step-by-step model of the transformation.

Advanced Learners

Have students use a computer drawing or paint program to show the progression of changes from rectangle to parallelogram. Reverse the steps to show a return to a rectangle. Show these steps in a slide show. Share with the class.

Solutions and Samples

4. Sample response:

Yes, because a rectangle is also a four-sided figure with opposite sides parallel.

Activity

Sample response:

The parallelogram is different from the rectangle because it has a different shape. It looks like the top of the rectangle has been shifted to the right to make the parallelogram. The figures are the same because they have the same base and the same area.

Hints and Comments

Materials

graph paper (one sheet per student) or index cards of 4 in. by 6 in. (one per student); scissors (one pair per student); tape (one roll per pair or group of students); transparency of graph paper, optional (one per class)

Overview

Students are introduced to the terms *quadrilateral* and *parallelogram*. Then they transform a rectangle in different parallelograms by cutting and pasting or taping.

The pictures in the Activity on page 15 of the Student Book show that a diagonal of a parallelogram divides the parallelogram into two congruent triangles. Therefore every triangle can be considered as half of a parallelogram.

This activity illustrates one of the properties of area: no matter how a shape is rearranged, the area of the shape remains the same. Students may not be aware that the height and base of each figure pictured in the Activity also remain the same. You might wait to explain these concepts and terms until students have finished problem 5 on the next page.

Planning

Discuss the term *quadrilateral* and give several examples. Also discuss the characteristics of a parallelogram. Ask students what they know about parallel lines and how they can determine whether lines are parallel or not. (Two parallel lines will always be equidistant from each other.) Students may work in pairs or in small groups on questions in the Activity. Discuss their findings.

Comments About the Solutions

Activity

Students will probably comment on the fact that the shapes formed by cutting and pasting look different than the original shape. When discussing this problem, ask students to explain what they know about the areas of the parallelograms. Most will respond that the areas are equal. A few students may notice that the bases and heights of the parallelograms are equal.

Notes

All of the parallelograms below enclose the same area.

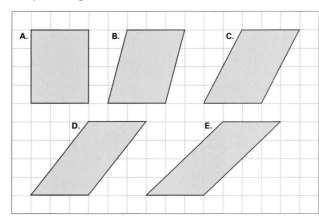

5 Relate these quadrilateral shapes and their identical areas to the Check Your Work problem 4 in Section A that deals with triangles.

5. a. In addition to having the same area, how are all the parallelograms shown here alike?

b. Describe how each of the parallelograms **B–E** could be transformed into figure **A**.

6. How can your method be used to find the area enclosed by any parallelogram?

6 Students may say that any parallelogram can be changed into a rectangle by cutting and taping triangular sections.

In Section A, you learned to **reshape** figures. You cut off a piece of a shape and taped that same piece back on in a different spot. If you do this, the area does not change.

Here are three parallelograms. The first diagram shows how to transform the parallelogram into a rectangle by cutting and taping.

7 Students may have more than one way to transform parallelograms **b** and **c** into rectangles.

7. Copy the other two parallelograms onto graph paper and show how to transform them into rectangles.

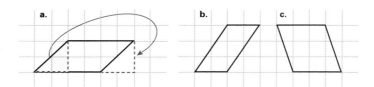

8 Be sure the labels are in square units.

8. Calculate the area of all three parallelograms.

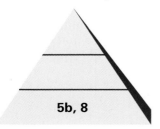
Reaching All Learners

Extension

Have students copy parallelogram B–E and transform them into rectangles on graph paper.

Advanced Learners

Provide graph paper and rulers and challenge students to create a parallelogram that has the same area as the quadrilaterals at the top of page 16 but is as long as the graph paper). This parallelogram would be very long and thin and would stretch across the page from top to bottom.

Solutions and Samples

5. a. They all have three units along the bottom and top, and they all are four units tall.

b. Answers will vary. Sample response:

Cut a triangular piece from the right side of the parallelogram and paste it onto the left side.

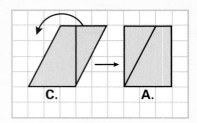

6. Answers will vary. Sample responses:

You can find the area enclosed by any parallelogram by changing it into a rectangle and then counting the number of squares in the figure.

Any parallelogram with a base measurement and height measurement equal to the length and width of a rectangle will enclose an area equal to that of the rectangle.

7.

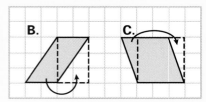

8. A. 8 square units (4 × 2 = 8 square units)

B. 6 square units (2 × 3 = 6 square units)

C. 9 square units (3 × 3 = 9 square units)

Hints and Comments

Materials

transparency of page 16 of the Student Book, optional (one per class);
graph paper (one sheet per student);
scissors, optional (one pair per student);
tape, optional (one roll per pair or group of students)

Overview

Students use the cutting and pasting strategy to transform parallelograms into a rectangle. They find a method to determine the areas enclosed by parallelograms.

About the Mathematics

The areas enclosed by most parallelograms can be found using the compensating strategy: cutting and pasting triangular sections of the parallelogram to reshape the figure into a rectangle. Applying this strategy to figure **E** is more difficult; the compensating strategy must be used twice. Note that the strategy of framing the parallelogram within a rectangle and subtracting the remaining parts can always be used.

Planning

Students may work on problems 5 and 6 in pairs or small groups and on problems 7 and 8 individually.

Comments About the Solutions

5. Some students may say that you can put the parallelogram straight up. Be aware that they may possibly think that the height will increase, as indicated below.

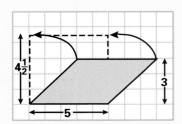

With this transformation, the enclosed area will always be larger than that which the original parallelogram encloses. The idea of shifting will be further developed on page 17 of the Student Book.

See more Hints and Comments on page 101.

Notes

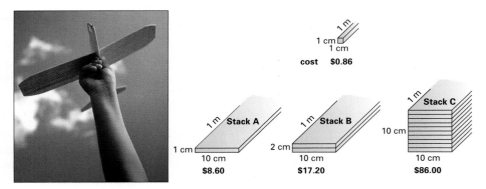

cost **$0.86**

Stack A
1 cm
10 cm
$8.60

Stack B
2 cm
10 cm
$17.20

Stack C
10 cm
10 cm
$86.00

Balsa is a lightweight wood used to make model airplanes. For convenience, balsa is sold in standard lengths. This makes it easy to calculate prices. The price of a board that is 1 meter (m) long, 1 centimeter (cm) wide, and 1 centimeter (cm) thick is $0.86. Jim priced each of the three stacks.

9. Explain how Jim could have calculated the price of each stack.

These boards are also 1 m long.

10.a. Estimate the price of the whole stack.

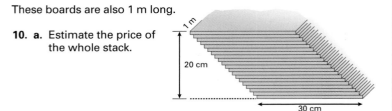

20 cm

30 cm

10a Compare the stack to Stack B (10 times taller and 3 times wider, or 30 times the cost of B). Or compare to Stack C (twice as tall and 3 times wider, or 6 times the cost of C).

b. Jim straightened the stack. Now it is much easier to see how to calculate the price. Calculate the price of this stack.

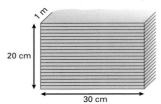

20 cm

30 cm

c. Compare this with your initial estimate.

10b Students may want to find the slanted dimension to find the area, but remind them that even our heights are always measured straight up and down, never slanted or leaning. Reason with students how this measurement would actually be longer than the true height.

Reaching All Learners

Intervention

If students have difficulty visualizing the context, it may be helpful to demonstrate this idea using a stack of rulers, books, or cuisenaire blocks. Use cuisenaire rods/flats to show the change from 1 rod to 1 flat to 1 cube. The length would not be accurate, but the height and width would be correct.

Extension

Have students explain how the slanted and straight stacks of boards relate to parallelograms and rectangles.

Solutions and Samples

9. Answers will vary. Sample response:

Stack **A** is made of 10 boards that measure

1 cm by 1 cm by 1 m. The price for one board this size is $.0.86, so the price for 10 boards is 10 × $0.86 = $8.60.

Stack **B** is made of two layers of stack **A**, so the price is 2 × $8.60 = $17.20.

Stack **C** is made of five layers of stack **B**, or

10 layers of stack **A**, so the price is 5 × $17.20, or 10 × $8.60 = $86.

10. a. Estimates will vary. Accept estimates between $450 and $600.

b. $516

Sample work:

The stack is three times as wide and twice as tall as stack **C** from problem 9, so I calculated 3 × 2 × $86 = $516.

c. Answers will depend on students' estimates from problem 10a.

Hints and Comments

Materials

rulers, optional (several per group)

Overview

Students explain how the prices for different stacks of balsa wood were determined. They estimate the price of a slanted stack of balsa wood and calculate the total price for the same stack after it has been straightened.

About the Mathematics

This context of straightening a stack of boards is intended to reinforce students' understanding of finding the area enclosed by a parallelogram. By comparing the slanted stack with the straightened stack, students may notice that only the width of the boards and the number of boards, or the height, determine the price of the stack. The concept of shifting to transform a parallelogram into a rectangle can be used to find a rule to determine the area of a parallelogram. The compensation strategy used in problem 5 can also be used to devise a rule or formula for finding the area enclosed by a parallelogram.

Planning

Students can work on problems 9 and 10 individually or in small groups. Discuss these problems, focusing on the idea behind the context of the slanted and straightened stacks, rather than on the computations involved.

Did You Know?

The wood of the balsa tree is remarkably light and strong and does not bend easily. It is one of the most rapidly growing trees of the tropical forests of Central and South America. The wood is lighter than cork. Ecuador grows most of the world's supply of balsa wood.

Notes

11 Discuss why B, C, and D are not parallelograms and what the numbers outside the rectangles mean.

(Note that $2\frac{1}{2} + 2\frac{1}{2} = 5$ units long; the $2\frac{1}{2}$ marking is not the tick mark, but the distance.)

Help students to recognize that each rectangle that encloses a quadrilateral has an area of 20 square units. Students who divide the quadrilaterals in $\frac{1}{2}$ or $\frac{1}{4}$ will quickly deduce that these divisions create triangles that have areas that are $\frac{1}{2}$ the area of the rectangle.

Reinforce the concept that a triangle has $\frac{1}{2}$ the area of a rectangle with the same base and height.

It is not easy to find the area of some quadrilaterals.

Here are four shaded quadrilaterals that are not parallelograms. Each one is drawn inside a rectangle. Every corner touches one side of the rectangle.

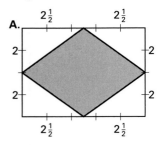

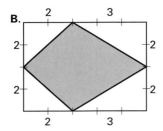

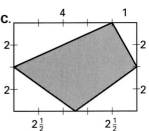

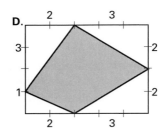

11. a. Use **Student Activity Sheet 9** to calculate the area of each shaded quadrilateral. Show your solution methods; you may describe them with words, calculations, or a drawing. Hint: It may be helpful to draw the gridlines inside the rectangles.

b. Try to think of a rule for finding the area of a quadrilateral whose corners touch the sides of a rectangle. Explain your rule.

12. a. On graph paper, draw eight different shapes, each with an area of five square units.

Assessment Pyramid

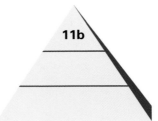

Generalize formulas and procedures for determining the areas of parallelograms.

Reaching All Learners

Extension

After problem 11, you may say, *Draw some other quadrilaterals on graph paper to see if your rule works.*

Parental Involvement

Problem 12 is a great homework challenge. Students can work with their parents to create as many polygons as possible with areas of 5 square units.

Advanced Learners

Have students draw a quadrilateral enclosed in a rectangle that does not have an area that is $\frac{1}{2}$ the rectangle's area. This activity may help to solidify the concept that one quadrilateral diagonal must be parallel to a side of the rectangle to have $\frac{1}{2}$ its area.

Solutions and Samples

11. a. **A.** 10 square units

    B. 10 square units

    C. 10 square units

    D. 10 square units

Strategies will vary. Students may subtract the areas of the corner triangles from the area of the rectangle.

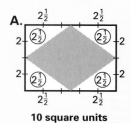
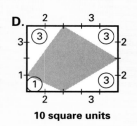

A. 10 square units   **B.** 10 square units

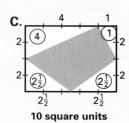
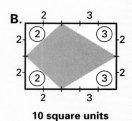

C. 10 square units   **D.** 10 square units

Students may divide the rectangle into smaller rectangles and use triangles to find the area.

b. Answers will vary. Sample student response:

When two corners of the quadrilateral are on **the same grid line**, then its area is half of the rectangle's area. Also see Comments About the Solutions for problems 11a and 11b.

12. a. Sample drawing:

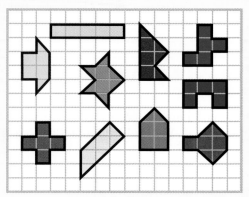

Hints and Comments

Materials
Student Activity Sheet 9 (one per student); graph paper (one sheet per student); rulers (one per student)

Overview
Students find the areas of quadrilaterals that are enclosed by rectangles. Students develop a rule for finding these areas. Then they draw eight different shapes on graph paper, each of which encloses an area of five square units.

Planning
Students can work on problems 11 and 12 in pairs or in small groups. Problem 11a might be done with the whole class together. Otherwise, be sure to discuss this problem before students continue with problems 11b and 12a. Problem 12 is continued on the next page.

Comments About the Solutions

11. a. You might want students to create diagrams that show their computations and strategies and share them during a class discussion. You might need to discuss the issue of units for these measurements. For example:

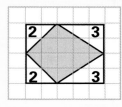 or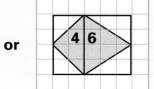

b. There is a rule that if a quadrilateral can be enclosed by a rectangle and it has at least one diagonal parallel to a side of the rectangle, the area of the quadrilateral will be half the area of the rectangle.

12. a. You may want students to check each other's shapes to see that the area each figure encloses is five square units. Students do not have to explicitly calculate areas to answer this problem.

B Area Patterns

Notes

12b Drawings by Jaime, Mike, and Jolene are unlike the quadrilaterals on p.18 because they do not have diagonals that are parallel to a side of the rectangle, so their areas are not $\frac{1}{2}$ of the enclosing rectangle.

12c Students may be asked to relate their triangle drawings to the triangle discoveries in the quadrilaterals on p.18. Remind students that rectangles could be turned into parallelograms.

13a Students may recognize that they do not need to worry about getting the right base or height number because the product will be the same.

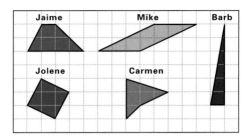

Jaime, Mike, Jolene, Carmen, and Barb drew these shapes.

> **b.** Did they all draw a shape with an area of five square units? Explain why or why not.
>
> **c.** Draw two triangles that have an area of five square units.

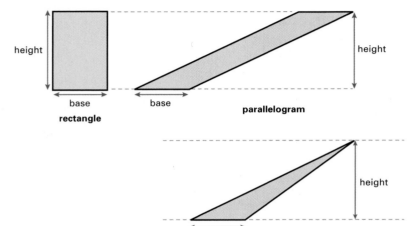

You worked with three shapes in this section. When you describe a rectangle, parallelogram, or triangle, the words **base** and **height** are important. The base describes how wide the figure is. The height describes how tall it is.

13. a. Use the words *base* and *height* to describe ways to find the areas of rectangles, parallelograms, and triangles. Be prepared to explain why your ways work.

b. Check whether your description for finding the area works by finding the area for some of the rectangles, parallelograms, and triangles in problems you did earlier in this section and in Section A.

c. Draw a triangle with base 4 and height 2. Now draw a triangle with base 2 and height 4. What observations can you make?

Assessment Pyramid

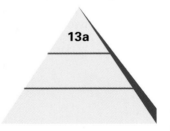

Generalize formulas and procedures for determining the areas of rectangles, triangles, and parallelograms.

Reaching All Learners

Vocabulary Building

Have students record the possible synonyms for *base* and *height* (for example, *length, width*) in their notebook. Remind students that area is labeled in square units.

Extension

For problem 13b, have students incorporate persuasive writing and draw examples to demonstrate their findings.

Solutions and Samples

12. b. No, only Jaime's and Jolene's two shapes have an area of 5 square units. Explanations will vary. Sample student explanations:

Jaime:

Divide the shape into three parts.

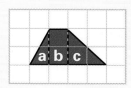

Area of part **a** = $\frac{1}{2} \times 2 \times 1 = 1$ square unit

Area of part **b** = 2 square units

Area of part **c** = $\frac{1}{2} \times 2 \times 2 = 2$ square units

Area = $1 + 2 + 2 = 5$ square units

Mike:

Draw a rectangle around it. The area of this rectangle is $7 \times 2 = 14$. Then subtract the area for the two triangles (the white space) which, when placed together, form a 2×4 rectangle.

Area = $14 - 8 = 6$ square units

Barb:

Draw a rectangle around it. The area of this rectangle is $1 \times 6 = 6$ square units. The area of my shape is half of this area, or 3 square units.

Jolene:

Draw a rectangle around it and find the area.

$A = 3 \times 3 = 9$ square units.
Then subtract the areas of the triangles,

$A = 9 - 4 = 5$ square units

Carmen:

Divide it into three triangles and a square.

$A = \frac{1}{2} + 1 + 1\frac{1}{2} + 1 = 4$ square units

c. Sample drawings:

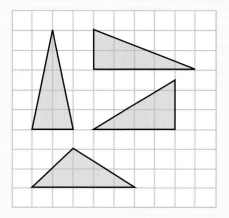

Hints and Comments

Materials

rulers, optional (one per student);
graph paper (one sheet per student);
scissors, optional (one pair per student);
tape, optional (one roll per pair or group of students);
transparency of graph paper, optional (one per class)

Overview

Students check whether five given shapes each has an area of five square units. Then they draw two different triangles that have an area of five square units. Students describe ways to find the areas of rectangles, parallelograms, and triangles.

About the Mathematics

It is more important for students to understand the concept of area as it relates to rectangles, parallelograms, and triangles than to use rules or formulas for finding the areas of these shapes.

Planning

Students can work on problems 12 and 13 in pairs or in small groups. Discuss the concepts of base and height.

See more Hints and Comments on page 102.

13. a. Answers will vary. Students' responses should include the following information:

The area of a rectangle is *base* times *height*.

The area of a parallelogram is *base* times *height*.

The area of a triangle is $\frac{1}{2}$ of *base* times *height*.

b. Answers will vary. Students should write the base and height of each shape, and calculate its area.

c. They have the same area because $\frac{1}{2} \times 4 \times 2$ is the same as $\frac{1}{2} \times 2 \times 4$.

B Area Patterns

Notes

Show the formulas in a variety of formats:

$A = b \times h$

$A = bh,$

$A = b \cdot h$

$A = l \times w$

$A = lw$

$A = l \cdot w$

Discuss which measurement is base and height or length and width. Then utilize the commutative property of multiplication to show that it won't make any difference in the area calculation if these two are switched when multiplied.

15a Note that a rectangle is also a parallelogram. If students have drawn a rectangle, discuss this issue. Show the triangle that can be created from your parallelogram and its area.

15b Show the parallelogram that can be created by doubling your triangle and its area.

Strategies and Formulas

The area enclosed by a parallelogram is the same as the area enclosed by a rectangle with the same base and height. You can find the area enclosed by any parallelogram using this formula.

The area (A) is equal to the base (b) times the height (h).

$$A_{\text{rectangle}} = b \times h$$

$$A_{\text{parallelogram}} = b \times h$$

A **triangle** is always half the size of some rectangle or a parallelogram. You can find the area enclosed by a triangle using this formula.

The area (A) is equal to one-half of the base (b) times the height (h).

$$A_{\text{triangle}} = \tfrac{1}{2}b \times h$$

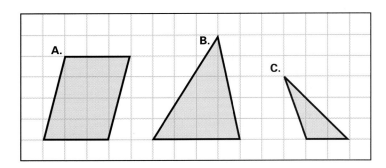

14. Calculate the area enclosed by these shapes.

15. a. On graph paper, draw a parallelogram that encloses an area of 8 square units.

   b. On graph paper, draw a triangle that encloses an area of 8 square units.

Assessment Pyramid

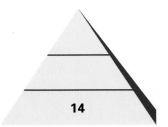

14

Compute the areas of geometric figures.

Reaching All Learners

Intervention

A triangle's area can be shown as $A =$ half of $b \times h$ or as $bh \div 2$, and this might be more clear for students with special needs.

Advanced Learners

Extend problem 15 for these students. Challenge them to find parallelograms or triangles of various sizes.

Solutions and Samples

14. A. The parallelogram encloses an area of:

$b \times h = 3 \times 4 = 12$ square units.

B. The triangle in the middle encloses an area of:

$\frac{1}{2} \times b \times h = \frac{1}{2} \times 4 \times 5 = 10$ square units.

C. The last triangle encloses an area of:

$\frac{1}{2} \times b \times h = \frac{1}{2} \times 2 \times 3 = 3$ square units.

15. a. Answers will vary. Sample measures of a parallelogram: base 2 and height 4 or vice versa.

b. Answers will vary. Sample measures for a triangle: base 4 and height 4 or base 2 and height 8 or vice versa.

Hints and Comments

Materials

graph paper (one sheet per student);
transparency of graph paper, optional (one per class)

Overview

Students are introduced to the formulas for finding the area of a rectangle, a parallelogram, and a triangle. They apply these formulas to three given shapes.

Planning

Have a short class discussion about the two area formulas introduced here. Students can work on problems 14 and 15 individually or in pairs. These problems can be used as informal assessment and/or assigned as homework.

Comments About the Solutions

14. Instead of using the formula, students can use more "informal" strategies. When discussing the answers and methods, be sure to include the use of the formulas as well. For the triangle, some students may take 3 as base instead of 2. This can be explained because the height is outside the triangle, which may be confusing. If you notice students making this mistake, relate the triangle's base and height to the parallelogram of which the triangle is half. This may help students recognize the appropriate height of the triangle:

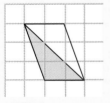

Notes

Students may need help understanding why base and height cannot be determined by simply counting the number of squares a side crosses.

For some triangles, the length of the base or height is not easy to establish. This is true for this triangle. Since the triangle is on a "slant," the grid doesn't help you find the length of the base and height.

16. Use a strategy to find the area enclosed by this "slanted" triangle.

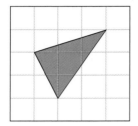

Miguel found the area enclosed by the triangle by drawing a square around it. Then he calculated the area of the three shaded triangles.

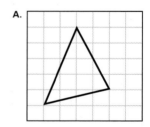

Area = ?

Area square = ?

Area = 3

Area orange triangle = ?

Area = ?

17. Finish Miguel's work. What is the area enclosed by the orange triangle?

17 and 18 Some students may only want to use reallotment to find the areas of the surrounding triangles. Work together and use the suggestion that is mentioned in the Comments About the Solutions to determine the area of the triangles that have to be subtracted from the rectangle that encloses the given triangle.

18. Copy these images on graph paper and use Miguel's strategy to find the area.

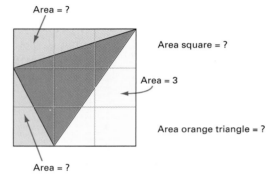

A.

B.

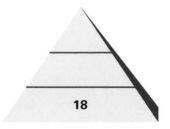
Reaching All Learners

Intervention

Help students understand the difference between distances along straight or slanted sides of a triangle and why you cannot just count the squares a side crosses to get a base or height measurement for a slanted triangle. Use an overhead transparency of a triangle (such as the one on page 21) and then rotate it so that the sides are along the grid squares. Students will then see that the slanted distance is longer. Create a statement about the side lengths of "slanted" sides on triangles.

Accommodation

Problem 18 has many steps. Break down the steps and retype a bulleted list of instructions for students to follow.

Solutions and Samples

16. Strategies may vary. One of the strategies is described in problem 17. Another strategy is the compensation method:

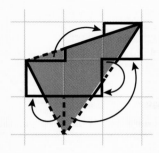

17. $3\frac{1}{2}$ square units. Strategies will vary.

Sample student response:

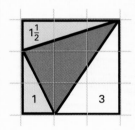

First Miguel found the area of the square.

$A = 3 \times 3 = 9$ square units

Then he found the areas of the triangles.

$\frac{1}{2} \times 2 \times 1 = 1$ square unit

$\frac{1}{2} \times 2 \times 3 = 3$ square units

$\frac{1}{2} \times 1 \times 3 = 1\frac{1}{2}$ square units

Then he added the areas of the triangles.

$1 + 3 + 1\frac{1}{2} = 5\frac{1}{2}$ square units

Finally he subtracted the areas of the triangles from the area of the square.

$A = 9 - 5\frac{1}{2} = 3\frac{1}{2}$ square units

18. A.

9 square units. Sample student work:

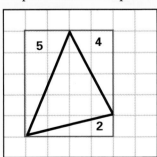

Area of enclosing rectangle: $4 \times 5 = 20$

Areas of parts to subtract: 4, 2, 5

Area of triangle: $20 - 4 - 2 - 5 = 9$ square units

Hints and Comments

Materials

graph paper (one sheet per student);
transparency of graph paper, optional (one per class)

Overview

Students use a strategy for finding the area of a triangle for which the formula can not easily be used. They see how the strategy of framing the triangle within a rectangle and subtracting the remaining parts is used.

Planning

Students can work on problems 16 and 17 in pairs or small groups and on problem 18 individually.

Comments About the Solutions

16. Encourage students to copy the triangle on graph paper.

17. Encourage students to copy Miguel's drawing on graph paper. They then can write the area of each triangle to be subtracted on their drawings. Some students will be confused when they draw rectangles around the outside triangles because the rectangles overlap:

You may suggest that students draw the triangles separately in order to focus on only one triangle in each drawing.

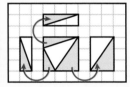

B.

$16\frac{1}{2}$ square units. Sample student work:

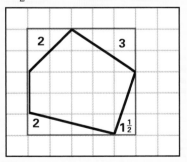

Area of enclosing rectangle: $5 \times 5 = 25$

Areas of parts to subtract: 2, 2, 3, $1\frac{1}{2}$

Area of shape: $25 - 2 - 2 - 3 - 1\frac{1}{2} = 16\frac{1}{2}$ square units

Notes

Note that the Summary uses only one parallelogram to demonstrate all of the strategies to find area.

 Area Patterns

Summary

In this section, you learned many ways to calculate the areas enclosed by a variety of shapes.

To find the area enclosed by this shape, you can use any of the following strategies.

1. Count the squares, cut, and tape partial units.

Count the number of complete squares inside the shape, cut out the remaining pieces, and move them to form new squares.

Step 1 **Step 2**

2. Reshape the figure.

Cut off larger parts of the original figure and tape them somewhere else.

Step 1 **Step 2**

3. Enclose the shape and subtract extras.

Draw a rectangle around the shape in such a way that you can easily subtract the areas that are not part of the shape.

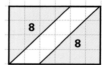

In this case, the area enclosed by the parallelogram is the area enclosed by the rectangle minus the areas of the two triangles.

24 − 8 − 8

The area is 8 square units.

Reaching All Learners

Parent Involvement

Use another parallelogram and have students use graph paper and work with their parents to show how to find the area using strategies 3–5 from the Summary.

Hints and Comments

Overview

Students read the Summary, which reviews the strategies for finding area enclosed by a shape. In the examples, the same parallelogram is used.

Planning

You may give students a shape different from the parallelogram used in the Summary and ask them to show all the strategies from the Summary using this shape. Or you may ask students to design other shapes that could be exchanged for the parallelogram used in the Summary. Students can then show how the five strategies can be used to determine the areas of the shapes they designed. Allow students to draw different shapes for each strategy if they want to.

Notes

Work in groups using poster paper to take a parallelogram or a triangle through all 5 area strategies and post the groups' work in the classroom. Students can pair with another group and share their work.

4. Double the shape or cut it in half.

The area of the green triangle is half the area enclosed by the corresponding rectangle (square).

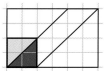

5. Use formulas.

You can use the relationship between a parallelogram and a rectangle.

> The area enclosed by a parallelogram is equal to the area enclosed by a rectangle with the same base and the same height.

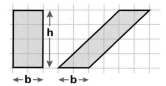

This relationship gives you the formula:

$$A_{\text{parallelogram}} = b \times h$$

For the areas enclosed by a rectangle and a triangle, you can also use formulas.

$$A_{\text{rectangle}} = b \times h$$

$$A_{\text{triangle}} = \tfrac{1}{2} b \times h$$

Reaching All Learners

Reflection

Ask, *Which area strategy is the easiest/most difficult for you to use? Why?* Have students list an advantage or disadvantage for each strategy.

Advanced Learners

Have students show a shape to two or three adults and ask them how they would find the area. Students can report their findings.

Hints and Comments

Overview

Students continue reading the Summary, which reviews the strategies for finding area enclosed by a shape.

Notes

Be sure to discuss Check Your Work with your students so they understand when to give themselves credit for an answer that is different than the one at the back of the book.

For Further Reflection

Reflective questions are meant to summarize and discuss important concepts.

B **Area Patterns**

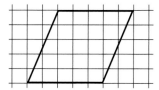

1. **a.** On **Student Activity Sheet 9**, shade a rectangle that encloses the same area as the parallelogram on the left.

   b. Use this parallelogram to shade a triangle on **Student Activity Sheet 9** that encloses an area half the area of the parallelogram.

2. Use **Student Activity Sheet 9** to determine the area of each of these shapes. Use any method.

A. 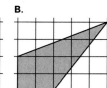 B. 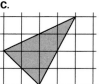 C. D.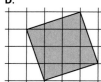

3. For each strategy described in the Summary, find an example of a problem from Section A or B where you used that strategy.

4. On graph paper, draw two different parallelograms and two different triangles each enclosing an area of 12 square units.

For Further Reflection

Which of the methods described in the Summary for finding the area of a shape do you think will be the most useful? Explain your reasoning.

Assessment Pyramid

☐ FFR

1, 2, 3, 4

Assesses Section B Goals

Reaching All Learners

Accommodation

For problem 3, give students the page and problem number and have them tell which strategy from the Summary pages is used to find the area.

Solutions and Samples

Answers to Check Your Work

1. a. You can have different drawings. Here is one possible drawing.

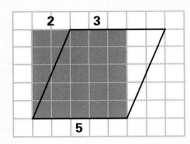

Make sure the area enclosed by your rectangle is 25 square units.

b. You can have different drawings. Here are three possible ones.

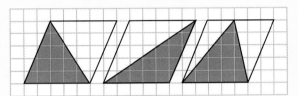

2. a. 10 square units

b. 9 square units

c. 6 square units

d. 10 square units

Compare the methods you used with the methods used by one of your classmates.

3. You may have used different strategies than your classmates. Possible answers:

- Count, cut, and paste partial units: Section A, problem 5H.

- Reshape the figure: Section A, problems 5E and F; Section B, problem 7.

- Enclose the shape and subtract: Section A, some shapes in problems 14 and 15.

- Double the shape or cut it in half: Section A, problem 4, some shapes in problems 14, 15; Section B, problem 13.

- Use formulas: Section B, problem 13.

4. You can have different answers. For example, you could have a parallelogram with base 3 and height 4, a parallelogram with base 6 and height 2, a triangle with base 6 and height 4, and one with base 8 and height 3. Have one of your classmates check your drawings by finding the area enclosed by each.

Hints and Comments

Overview

Students use the Check Your Work problems as self-assessment. The answers to these problems are also provided on Student Book pages 71 and 72.

Planning

After students complete Section B, you may assign as homework appropriate activities from the Additional Practice section, located on Student Book page 65.

For Further Reflection

Students' preferences may vary. Have students share their ideas in class.

Section Focus

The instructional focus of Section C is to:

- develop students' understanding of which units and tools are appropriate to estimate and measure length and area;
- develop students' understanding of and ability to use relations between units of measure within the metric system and within the customary system; and
- compare, estimate, and compute areas using metric and customary measuring units.

Pacing and Planning

Day 9: Going Metric		Student pages 25–28
INTRODUCTION	Problem 1	Identify objects that are a centimeter, meter, and kilometer in length.
CLASSWORK	Problems 2–5	Investigate the use of metric and customary units to measure length and area.
ACTIVITY	Activity, page 27 Problem 6	Measure a square whose sides are one meter.
HOMEWORK	Problem 7	Find relationships among metric and customary square units of measure.

Day 10: Area (Continued)		Student pages 28–31
INTRODUCTION	Problem 8	Find relationships among metric and customary square units of measure.
CLASSWORK	Problems 9–14	Determine the number of square meters of marble needed to cover three floors and multiply mixed fractions using the area of a rectangle as a model.
HOMEWORK	Problem 15	Determine the number of tiles (10 cm by 10 cm) needed to cover floors.

Day 11: Hotel Lobby		Student pages 32–36
INTRODUCTION	Review homework.	Review homework from Day 10.
CLASSWORK	Problem 16	Determine the cost of covering a rectangular area with different types of floor covering.
HOMEWORK	Check Your Work For Further Reflection	Student self-assessment: Count, estimate, and compute the area for various figures.

Additional Resources: Additional Practice, Section C, page 66

Materials

Student Resources

Quantities listed are per student.

- **Student Activity Sheets 10** and **11**

Teachers Resources

No resources required

Student Materials

Quantities listed are per student, unless otherwise noted.

- Centimeter graph paper (one sheet)
- Centimeter rulers
- Inch rulers
- Meter sticks (one per group of students)
- Scissors
- Self-stick note (two per group of students)

* See Hints and Comments for optional materials.

Learning Lines

Measuring Units

In this section, students use metric and customary units of measure. The difference between a linear unit of measure and a square unit of measure is addressed. The metric system is based on refinements in tenths. One millimeter is a refinement of one centimeter; it is one-tenth of a centimeter. Students studied refinements of units of measure within the metric system (meter, decimeter, and centimeter) in the unit *Models You Can Count On.* Studying metric units helps students develop an understanding of decimal numbers.

Length

Every student should have an idea about the relative sizes of one centimeter, one meter, and so on, in order to estimate lengths and to convert between metric units. For example, if students have points of reference for one meter and one centimeter, they can estimate that there are 100 centimeters in one meter. 1 centimeter: Your thumbnail is about 1 centimeter wide, which is smaller than one inch.

Area

To have an idea about the relative sizes of one square centimeter, one square meter, and so on, the dimensions of the shape are used. The relationships between square units of different sizes can be found by calculating how many smaller units fit into each larger unit. For example, one square meter has 100 rows of 100 square centimeters; therefore, a total of 100×100 square centimeters fit inside a square meter. In the same way, the relationships between customary square units of measure can be found: in one square yard, three rows of three square feet will fit; so one square yard is nine square feet. Students do not convert between the metric and customary systems.

Area Model

Finding the areas of rectangular floors with sides that are partly fractional, pre-formally addresses the multiplication of mixed numbers and fractions. This method is later used in other contexts for multiplying fractions, for example, in the context of probability, and is referred to as the area model. Using the area of a rectangle as a model to multiply mixed numbers is made explicit in the unit *Facts and Factors.* For example, to calculate $2\frac{1}{2} \times 3\frac{1}{2}$, a drawing of a rectangle of $2\frac{1}{2}$ by $3\frac{1}{2}$ is used as a model.

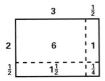

At the End of This Section: Learning Outcomes

Students are able to use measurement units and tools appropriately for lengths and areas. Students know and can use relations between units of measure within the metric system and within the customary system.

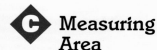

Measuring Area

Notes

Discuss the two measurement systems: customary (US) vs. metric (most of the rest of the world).

Display a meter stick with *cm* and *mm* identified or sample lengths of *m*, *cm*, and *mm*. Discuss prefixes on the metric base units of *meter*, *liter*, and *gram* and how these relate to the number 10.

Display pictures or length examples that compare:

- 1 cm to 1 in.
- 1 m to 1 yd
- 1 km to 1 mi (maps)

List all of the metric units students have ever heard and the context in which they were used.

Measuring Area

Going Metric

Metric units are easy to use because the relationship between units is based on multiples of 10. The United States is one of the few countries that still uses the customary system of measurement.

Today, Americans are buying and selling products from other countries. You might notice that many products in the grocery store, such as bottled water and canned fruits, are measured in metric units. If you run track, you probably measure distance using meters. International games, such as the Olympics, use metric distances. Medicines are weighed in metric units. Food labels usually list fat, protein, and carbohydrates in metric units.

Here are some descriptions to help you understand and remember the sizes of some commonly used metric units for length.

Length

1 centimeter: Your thumbnail is about 1 centimeter wide, which is smaller than one inch.

1 meter: One giant step is about 1 meter long, which is a little more than one yard.

1 kilometer: The length of about ten football fields is about 1 kilometer, which is about 0.6 of a mile.

Reaching All Learners

Vocabulary Building

Have students put *m*, *cm*, *km* into the vocabulary section of their notebook with a definition and illustration, write out the words these abbreviations stand for, and describe or draw a point of reference for each one..

Intervention

List customary or metric units and a common benchmark for comparison.

Hints and Comments

Materials

centimeter rulers (one per student);
meter sticks (one per group of students)

Overview

Students review their understanding of metric units and start to develop points of reference for one centimeter, one meter, and one kilometer.

There are no problems to solve on this page.

About the Mathematics

The development of points of reference for units of measurement is very important for students, whether the units are English or metric.

Planning

You might begin this section reading Student Book page 25 together as a class and have a discussion of the metric system. To demonstrate the length of one meter, have students extend their arms until the distance between their hands is about one meter or hold one hand at a distance of one meter from the floor. To show the size of one centimeter, have students examine the width of one of their fingernails. Then discuss other points of reference; for example, the height of a door is about two meters; a city block is about 150 meters long.

Some students may have experience in track. To compare the lengths of one kilometer and one mile, have these students recall that when running on a 400-meter track:

1 mile = 4 laps + 9 meters (about 9 yards, or 27 feet)

1 kilometer = $2\frac{1}{2}$ laps

◆ Measuring Area

Notes

1 and 4 Have students work on these lists in groups first. Then have the class prepare a combined list with illustrations to put up in the room. For the rest of this section, students should be encouraged to add to (or delete from) the list.

2 Combine other metric statements and post them.

$1 \text{ cm}^2 = 1$ square cm

These are equivalent labels, but be careful that students do not use "1^2 cm." Discuss how this label is different from 1 cm^2.

4d Square km is the hardest to learn because students may seriously underestimate or over-estimate the size of a square km. A map of the local area may help with this size.

---

1. Make a list of things that are approximately the size of:

   a. a centimeter

   b. a meter

   c. a kilometer

You probably worked with the metric system before. See if you can remember the answers to the following problems.

2. a. How many centimeters are in a meter?

   b. How many meters are in a kilometer?

   c. Write two other statements about how metric units relate to each other.

Area

One metric measuring unit for area is the square centimeter. The dimensions of the small square are exactly 1 cm by 1 cm. The area can be written as 1 cm^2.

An example of a customary measuring unit for area is a square inch (in^2).

3. a. Draw this measuring unit in your notebook.

   b. About how many square centimeters do you need to cover one square inch?

4. Give an example of something that is about the size of:

   a. a square centimeter

   b. a square inch

   c. a square meter

   d. a square kilometer

Reaching All Learners

Intervention

You are building an understanding of length and area (size of the square shape), so do not rush through this page. Students need many examples to build a foundation in metrics.

Parent Involvement

For problems 1 and 4, parents can help students add to their lists by finding household examples.

Accommodation

Provide cut-outs or samples of square m, square cm, square mm, square in., square ft, square yd.

Solutions and Samples

1. a. Answers will vary. Sample responses:
  - the width of a paper clip
  - the width of a pen

b. Answers will vary. Sample student responses:
  - the width of a door
  - four dictionaries lined up lengthwise

c. Answers will vary. Sample responses:
  - the distance between my house and my friend's house
  - the length of the fence around the playground
  - a 100-story building

2. a. 100 centimeters

b. 1,000 meters

c. Answers will vary. Sample responses:
  - There are ten centimeters in one decimeter.
  - There are ten decimeters in one meter.

3. a.

b. About six square centimeters.

4. a. Answers will vary. Sample responses:
  - a child's thumbnail
  - a button on a telephone
  - the head of a thumbtack

b. Answers will vary. Sample responses:
  - a stamp
  - an eraser

c. Answers will vary. Sample responses:
  - a tabletop
  - an unfolded road map
  - two bed pillows

d. Answers will vary. Sample responses:
  - 200 football fields
  - the land needed for a large shopping mall (including parking lots)

Hints and Comments

Materials
centimeter rulers (one per student);
meter sticks (one per group of students);
inch rulers (one per student)

Overview
Students find points of reference for one centimeter, one meter, and one kilometer. They review relationships among these measurement units. Then they investigate measuring units for area, like one square centimeter, one square inch, one square meter, and one square kilometer.

About the Mathematics
Every student should have an idea about the relative sizes of one centimeter, one meter, and so on, in order to estimate the sizes of objects and to convert between metric units. For example, if students have points of reference for one meter and one centimeter, they can estimate that there are 100 centimeters in one meter. Students may remember conversions between measures of length within the metric system from the unit *Models You Can Count On.*

Planning
Students may work in pairs or in small groups on problems 1–4.

Comments About the Solutions

1.–4.
Students' responses will demonstrate their prior knowledge about the relative sizes of different metric units. You may discuss the fact that a larger measuring unit of the metric system is always a multiple of ten of a smaller unit. For example, if you have one meter, then a smaller unit fits either 10, or 100, or 1,000 times in it. Points of references can be used to see that one centimeter doesn't fit 10 or 1,000 times in one meter, so it must be 100 times.

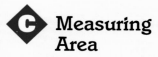
Measuring Area

Notes

You know that a shape that is one square meter in area does not have to be a square. You worked through many examples in Sections A and B where a shape was changed but the area stayed the same. You created a tessellation by cutting and pasting parts in different locations, while keeping the area the same.

Here are a variety of shapes that enclose an area of one square centimeter.

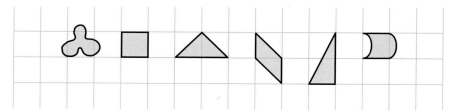

5 Try this individually and then share in groups to show many examples.

5. On graph paper, draw two different shapes that enclose an area of 1 square centimeter.

Many different types of square units are used to measure area, such as square meters, square centimeters, square yards, or square feet. If you need to measure an area more precisely, you often use smaller square units to measure the same space.

Activity

Use masking tape to define the square meter space. Leave this defined space and label it in the classroom as a reference.

 **Activity**

Draw 1 cm², on a self-stick note.
(Be sure the backside of the square is sticky.)

Cut out your square centimeter.

Have a group of four students use a meter stick and four centimeter squares to mark the four corners of a square whose sides measure 1 m, as in the sketch.

Note that this sketch is not drawn to scale!

6 Discuss the abbreviations of the square units; for example, one square meter can be written as 1 m².

6. What is the area of this figure in square meters?

Assessment Pyramid

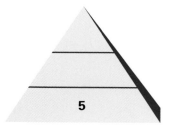

5

Compare the areas of shapes using a variety of strategies and measuring units.

Reaching All Learners

Accommodation

Use the floor (if tiled) or a wall (if bricks) to help with aligning the sticky notes.

Solutions and Samples

5. Answers will vary. Students can use what they learned about tessellations in Section A—what is taken away from one place must be made up for in another place"—to design other shapes that are 1 square centimeter.

6. One square meter

Hints and Comments

Materials

centimeter graph paper (one sheet per student); centimeter rulers (one per student); self-stick note (two per group of students); meter stick (one per group of students); scissors (one pair per student)

Overview

Students create two different shapes that enclose an area of one square centimeter. Then they mark out a square whose sides are one meter.

Planning

You might read and discuss the text at the top of Student Book page 27 as a class activity. Then have students work on problem 5 in small groups.

For the activity, students work preferably in groups of four. Two students can share one self-stick note and cut it in half, so each student can draw and cut out one square centimeter. Keep the marked square meters available for students who may need them to solve the problems on the next page.

Comments About the Activity

The activity is meant to give students an idea about the actual size of one square meter.

Notes

This drawing represents your square figure with side lengths of 1 m.

You can fill the square figure with smaller squares.

In this drawing, the figure is being filled along the bottom row. Each small square represents an area of 1 cm². Note that the squares are very, very small—you can barely see them, but they are there.

7c This would be a good time to reinforce short-cut multiplication (100 × 100) and the $A = b \times h$ formula that is used in problems 7 and 8.

7. **a.** How many square centimeters do you need to completely fill the bottom row? (Think about the relationship between meters and centimeters.)

b. How many rows are needed to fill the whole square?

c. What is the area of the figure in square centimeters? How did you calculate this?

d. You found the area of this square using two different units, first using square meters and then using square centimeters.
If you could choose, which units would you prefer to use for the area of this square? Explain your choice.

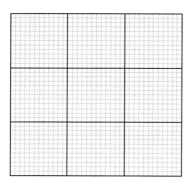

Area can also be measured using the customary measurement system.

8 Models of square inch, square foot, and square yard will help students compare and answer.

A drawing can be used to compare square inches and square yards. Here is a square with side lengths 1 yard long; it is not drawn in its actual size.

8. **a.** What is the area of the figure in square inches?

b. What is the area of the figure in square yards?

c. What is the area of the figure in square feet?

Assessment Pyramid

8abc

Compare the areas of shapes using a variety of strategies and measuring units.

Reaching All Learners

Accommodation

Students may need to use calculators to do problem 8.

Hands-On Learning

Use a meter stick to show the 100 cm needed across one side of the square meter.

Solutions and Samples

7. a. 100 square centimeters.

  b. 100 rows (the bottom row plus 99 more).

  c. 10,000 square centimeters.

    Possible methods:

- 100 rows of 100 squares is $100 \times 100 = 10{,}000$ square centimeters.
- use the formula: *area of rectangle* $= b \times h$ and multiply 100 cm $\times$ 100 cm.

  d. Answers will vary. Make sure students give reasons for their choice of units.

8. a. 1,296 square inches

  b. 1 square yard

  c. 9 square feet

Hints and Comments

Materials

yard sticks, optional (one per group of students); inch ruler, optional (one per student); calculators, optional

Overview

Students investigate and find relationships among metric and customary square units of measure.

About the Mathematics

The relationship among square units is found by covering a larger unit with smaller ones. In this way, the concept of area is reviewed: the number of measuring units that are needed to cover a shape.

Planning

Students may work on problems 7 and 8 in small groups. Have students explain their answers to problem 8.

Comments About the Solutions

7. and 8.
  The illustrations on Student Book page 28 are not drawn to scale so they do not show the actual sizes.

7. For some students, it may be helpful to use their actual square meter from the Activity on the previous page in order to find the answers.

8. To give students an idea about the actual size of one square yard, you might allow students to do the same tape outline as with the square meter. Some students may need to actually see the square yard in order to find the relationships among square yard, square feet, and square inches.

C Measuring Area

Notes

9 Expand this problem:

1 sq km = _____ sq m

1 sq m = _____ sq cm

1 sq yd = _____ sq ft

1 sq ft = _____ sq in.

A drawing of the larger square unit can help you find the area in a smaller unit of measure. You can imagine filling the larger square with smaller squares. You only need to remember the relationship between units, such as:

1 meter = 100 centimeters 1 kilometer = 1,000 meters

1 yard = 3 feet 1 foot = 12 inches 1 yard = 36 inches

You can use this information to figure out the relationship. If you forget, you can always recreate filling the larger space with smaller squares.

9. Complete the following:

a. 1 square meter =_____ square centimeters

b. 1 square yard = _____ square inches

10. a. **Reflect** Which units of measure are easier to use, metric units, like the meter and centimeter, or customary units, like the yard and inch? Explain your choice.

b. What units of measure would you use to find:

i. the length of a fruit fly?

ii. the distance a frog hops?

iii. the area of a soccer field?

iv. the area of your tabletop?

Assessment Pyramid

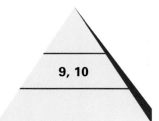

9, 10

Use metric and customary square units of measure appropriately.

Use relationships and points of reference.

Reaching All Learners

Extension

Have students find more examples like problem 10b and decide on the appropriate units. These can then be used for class review or a quiz.

Solutions and Samples

9. a. 1 square meter = 10,000 square centimeters

   b. 1 square yard = 9 square feet = 1,296 square inches

10. a. Answers will vary. Make sure students give reasons for their choice of units.

   b. Sample responses:

   i. millimeters or centimeters

   ii. centimeters or inches

   iii. square meters or square yards

   iv. square centimeters, square meters, square inches, or square feet

Hints and Comments

Overview

Students use their previous knowledge and experience to explore relationships within both metric and customary square units of measure.

Planning

You may have students work on problems 9 and 10 individually or in small groups. Have a class discussion about students' responses to problem 10.

C Measuring Area

Notes

Floor Covering

Several floors at Hotel Baron will be covered with Italian marble. The marble comes in squares that are exactly 1 m². Leftover pieces will not be wasted; they will be cut to fit spaces where a whole tile will not fit.

Here is one Italian marble tile.

These three floors will be covered with Italian marble.

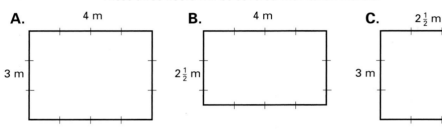

A. 4 m / 3 m **B.** 4 m / $2\frac{1}{2}$ m **C.** $2\frac{1}{2}$ m / 3 m

11 Some students may multiply the dimensions of the floor to find the area (A = *b* × *h*). Changing fractions to decimals is logical, but there is another way to eliminate both fractions and decimals: change units. This strategy is presented on the next page.

11. How many square meters of marble are needed for each of these floors? Show your calculations.

This floor needs to be covered with marble as well.

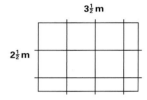

$3\frac{1}{2}$ m

$2\frac{1}{2}$ m

Robert used the formula you learned in the previous section to calculate the area of this floor.

$$A_{rectangle} = base \times height$$

Here is his work:

$$\text{Area floor} = 3\frac{1}{2} \times 2\frac{1}{2} \text{ m}^2$$

12. How would you calculate $3\frac{1}{2} \times 2\frac{1}{2}$?

Reaching All Learners

Accommodation

Have students use calculators to multiply mixed numbers (convert to decimals).

Provide graph paper to figure the floor areas. Reinforce the different strategies to find areas (Summary Section B). Students share methods aloud using a transparency.

Extension

Have students find the areas of many floors like the ones on this page in both metric and customary measurements.

Solutions and Samples

11. A. 12 m²

   B. 10 m²

   C. $7\frac{1}{2}$ m²

12. Answers will differ. Some students may write the numbers as decimals and use a calculator to calculate 2.5 × 3.5. The answer is 8.75.

   Some students may use the strategy that is used in problem 13 on the next page and get $8\frac{3}{4}$.

Hints and Comments

Materials

calculators, optional

Overview

Given that one marble tile is a square of one square meter, students determine the number of square meters of marble needed to cover three floors.

Students start to multiply mixed fractions using the area of a rectangle as a model.

About the Mathematics

Some students may multiply the dimensions of the floors (some of which involve fractions) to calculate the areas. Other students may simply count the numbers of squares to find the areas. Using the area of a rectangle as a model to multiply fractions is made explicit in the unit *Facts and Factors*.

The area $(2\frac{1}{2} \times 3\frac{1}{2})$ can be calculated as follows:

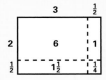

Area $= 6 + 1 + 1\frac{1}{2} + \frac{1}{4} = 8\frac{3}{4}$ square units

Planning

Students may work in pairs or in small groups on problems 11 and 12. Discuss students' answers to these problems.

Comments About the Solutions

11. Different strategies can be used to find the number of tiles needed. Some students may count the number of whole tiles and then combine two half tiles to make one whole tile.

12. Allow students to make up any strategy, even using a calculator. Some students may use the drawing and find for the number of tiles: six whole tiles, five half tiles, and one-fourth of a tile. Encourage these students to write this answer as a whole number of tiles and a fraction of a tile.

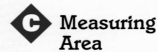 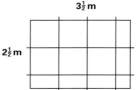
Notes

13 and 14 Use graph paper.

Robert didn't remember how to multiply these numbers.

Aisha helps Robert. She marks up the drawing of the floor to explain how to multiply these numbers.

13. How can Aisha's drawing be used to find the answer to $3\frac{1}{2} \times 2\frac{1}{2}$? Show your work.

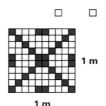

The hotel has two additional floors to cover with marble.

The hallway floor is $1\frac{1}{2}$ m wide by 8 m long.

The sitting room floor is $3\frac{1}{2}$ m by $5\frac{1}{2}$ m.

14. Calculate the area of both floors. Making a drawing like Aisha's may help you.

Another type of marble tile is available in smaller squares; each edge is 10 cm long.

These smaller tiles come in different colors. Arranging these colored tiles produces different floor patterns.

15. **a.** How many small tiles make up this larger square meter?

b. How many small tiles do you need to cover this floor?

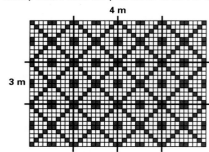

c. How many small tiles do you need to cover the floor from problem 12?

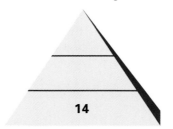
Reaching All Learners

Extension

Have students use square dm tiles to cover the hallway, floors, and sitting room in problem 14.

Solutions and Samples

13. $6 + 2\frac{1}{2} + \frac{1}{4}$ is $8\frac{3}{4}$ square meters.

Sample explanation: You can now count the whole squares and the parts of squares. There are 6 whole squares of 1 square meter, 5 half squares of $\frac{1}{2}$ square meter each, and one small part which is $\frac{1}{4}$ of a square meter. So you just add up the areas.

14. The area of the $1\frac{1}{2}$-by-8-meter floor is 12 square meters.

Sample calculation:

You have eight whole square meters and eight half square meters, which are four whole square meters. So the total is $8 + 4 = 12$ square meters.

The area of the $3\frac{1}{2}$-by-$5\frac{1}{2}$-meter floor is $19\frac{1}{4}$ square meters.

Sample calculation:

You have 15 whole square meters, eight half square meters, and a little piece of $\frac{1}{4}$ of a square meter, so together you have $15 + 4 + \frac{1}{4} = 19\frac{1}{4}$ square meters.

15. a. $10 \times 10 = 100$ smaller tiles.

b. 1,200 smaller tiles. Students may use the answer from problem 15a and reason that each large tile is replaced by 100 smaller ones. So $12 \times 100 = 1,200$ tiles are needed. Another way of reasoning is: the length of the floor will be 40 small tiles, and the width will be 30 small tiles. So $40 \times 30 = 1,200$ small tiles.

c. 875 small tiles. Sample strategies:

- There are six whole square meters, so they each can be covered by 100 small tiles ($6 \times 100 = 600$). You also have five half square meters, each of which can be covered by 50 small tiles ($5 \times 50 = 250$). And you have one fourth of a square meter left, which can be covered by 25 small tiles. Altogether you have $600 + 250 + 25$ small tiles, which is 875.

- You have 25 rows of 35 tiles, and $25 \times 35 = 875$.

- You can use the answer from problem 12 and multiply by 100 small tiles per square meter.
$8\frac{3}{4} = 8.75 \times 100 = 875$.

Hints and Comments

Materials

graph paper, optional (one sheet per student)

Overview

Students calculate the area of floors that have mixed fractions as side lengths. Then they use smaller tiles of 10 cm by 10 cm to cover floors.

About the Mathematics

In the context of money, you can get rid of the decimal point when converting the amounts into cents. This idea of changing units can be used when side lengths are not a whole number of meters. Converting from meters into decimeters may have the same effect; for example, $3\frac{1}{2}$ meters or 3.5 meters is the same as 35 decimeters. In problem 15, students informally change units when they cover the floor with smaller tiles that have side lengths of one decimeter. They actually count the number of square decimeters that cover the floor.

Planning

You may have students work on problems 13–15 individually or in small groups. Problem 14 may be used as informal assessment, and problem 15 may be assigned as homework. Discuss students' answers and strategies. For problem 15, depending on students' experiences with metric units, you may discuss the relationships between meters and decimeters, and square meters and square decimeters.

Comments About the Solutions

14. For the hallway, students may use a sketch and draw in the squares to find this out, or students may use the formula $b \times h$ and calculate $8 \times 1\frac{1}{2}$. For the sitting room, students may use the formula and a calculator; however, encourage students to make a drawing on graph paper like the one in problem 13.

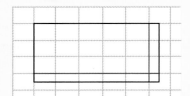

Notes

Discuss how you could cover this floor. Ask, *Are there any factors that need to be considered when putting in floor covering?* (durability, longevity, traffic amount, padding, and so on) *Would you rather have many seams or fewer seams? Why? How does cost relate to the number of seams?*

Hotel Lobby

14 yd

Floor Lobby

6 yd

The lobby of a new hotel is 14 yards long and 6 yards wide.

Reaching All Learners

Extension

Have students measure their bedroom or another room in their house and figure its area.

Hands-On Learning

To get an idea of the size of the hotel lobby, students could use a yardstick to measure the length and width of the lobby at the entrance to the school or the gym.

Hints and Comments

Overview

To get a better sense of the size of the hotel lobby, students could use a yard stick or measuring tape to mark of the length and width of the lobby in a large open area, such as the school cafeteria or gymnasium.

Measuring Area

Notes

Discuss what "waste" means when installing a floor covering and how this relates to the hotel floor covering.

16 Figure out one of the floor coverings together as a class and then send students into group work. Be sure students know that cost is a factor and that as little waste as possible is desired.

The owners are considering three options for covering the floor of the lobby: carpet (which comes in two widths of 3 yards or 4 yards) or vinyl. The current prices of each type of floor covering are shown below. Note that the carpet comes in two widths; 3 yards or 4 yards.

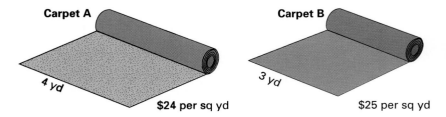

Carpet A
4 yd
$24 per sq yd

Carpet B
3 yd
$25 per sq yd

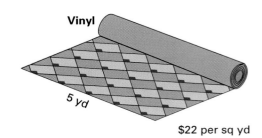

Vinyl
5 yd
$22 per sq yd

You are the salesperson for a floor-covering company. The hotel manager asks you to show with scale drawings how the lobby can be covered with each type of floor covering and to calculate the price for each of the three options for covering the lobby floor. Finally, you are asked to make a purchase recommendation.

16. Use **Student Activity Sheets 10** (with scale drawings of the lobby floor) and **11** to help you write a report that analyzes each floor option. Draw a picture of how each option could be laid out and calculate the price for each example. Don't forget to include a recommendation for the best choice of floor covering and your reasons for making this choice.

Assessment Pyramid

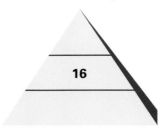

16

Understand the structure and use of the customary system of measurement.

Reaching All Learners

Intervention

Model the rolls using adding machine tape cut to scale for the appropriate widths and create a model of the 14 in. by 6 in. floor space.

Extension

Have students use the three options to figure out their bedroom floor covering and write a paragraph explaining which floor covering they selected and why.

Advanced Learners

Have students contact a floor covering company to find out the longevity of the three options and which option they would recommend for a hotel lobby. Then they report their findings.

Solutions and Samples

16. Some students will recommend the vinyl flooring because it is the most economical. Other students might recommend carpet B because it requires the fewest number of cuts (and seams). Answers will vary. Sample response:

The area of the lobby is 84 square yards

($14 \times 6 = 84$ yd^2). Using carpet A will cost \$2,016 ($84 \times \$24$ per yd^2). Two ways to lay carpet A are shown in this diagram. You can see that there's no waste.

Carpet A

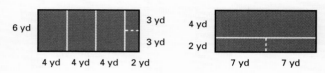

Using carpet B will cost \$2,100 ($84 \times \$25$ per yd^2). Two ways to place carpet B are shown in this diagram. There's no waste using this material either.

Carpet B

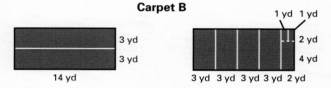

Here are two ways to use the vinyl flooring. If you choose the way shown on the left below, you need 3 strips (5 yards wide and 6 yards long), or 90 square yards. This way costs \$1,980 ($90 \times \$22$ per yd^2), and 6 square yards are wasted.

Using the way shown on the right below, you need 1 strip 5 yards wide and 14 yards long, or 70 square yards. You also need 3 strips (5 yards long and 1 yard wide), or 15 square yards. The total for this floor covering is 85 square yards, so the cost is \$1,870 (85×22 per yd^2), and one square yard is wasted.

Vinyl

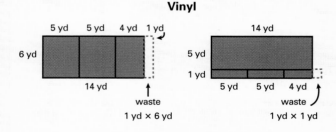

Hints and Comments

Materials

Student Activity Sheets 10 and **11** (one of each per student);
scissors (one pair per student);
adding machine tape, optional

Overview

Students investigate different options for covering the floor of a lobby. They also find the total cost of each floor covering.

Planning

You may want students to work on problem 16 in pairs or small groups so they can help each other. You may use this problem to assess groups of students. Briefly discuss students' answers.

Comments About the Solutions

16. Buying floor covering involves making decisions about how much of each covering must be purchased (depending on the width of the floor covering and the area of the room). Students must also consider the costs of the floor coverings.

You may want to emphasize different strategies for finding total costs. For example, students can compute the price of the carpet per yard length ($4 \times \$24 = \$96$), find out how many yard lengths are needed ($6 + 6 + 6 + 3 = 21$ yards), and then compute the total cost ($21 \times \$96 = \$2,016$).

Another strategy is to find the number of square yards that are needed and compute the total costs ($84 \times \$24 = \$2,016$). This strategy will not work if students have covered the floor in such a way that there is some leftover floor covering. In this case, the cost of the leftover covering must be included in the total cost.

Notes

After reading the Summary aloud, you may wish to have students extend the chart with personal examples of length and area in both systems of measurement. Also, they can write the area labels in more than one way (square inches, sq in., or in²).

Discuss and show the ways the area of a floor with mixed number dimensions could be figured.

$A = 12 + 2 + 1\frac{1}{2} + \frac{1}{4} = 15\frac{3}{4}$ m² (area model)

$A = 4.5 \times 3.5 = 15.75$ m² (decimals)

Summary

Two different systems of measurement are the *metric system* and the *customary system*. Each system uses different measuring units for length and area.

	Length	Area
Customary	inches	square inches
	feet	square feet
	yards	square yards
	miles	square miles
Metric	centimeters	square centimeters
	meters	square meters
	kilometers	square kilometers

To become more familiar with these units, it helps to make a list of things that are about the size of the unit. For example, a meter is like a giant step, a little more than a yard. A kilometer is about the distance you walk in ten minutes; to walk a mile takes about 15 minutes.

One square kilometer can be filled with smaller squares, for example, square meters.

Since 1 km = 1,000 m, one row would take up 1,000 m². There would be 1,000 rows, so the entire square kilometer would take one million square meters to completely cover it up (1,000 × 1,000 = 1,000,000).

Finding Area

To calculate or estimate area you can make a drawing, use a formula, or reposition pieces.

Here is one example.

The drawing shows that 12 whole tiles, seven half tiles (or $3\frac{1}{2}$ whole tiles), and $\frac{1}{4}$ of a tile are necessary to cover the floor.

Together $12 + 3\frac{1}{2} + \frac{1}{4} = 15\frac{3}{4}$ tiles, so the area of the floor is $15\frac{3}{4}$ m².

$4\frac{1}{2}$ m

$3\frac{1}{2}$ m

Reaching All Learners

Parental Involvement

Have students discuss the Summary with their parents. Students can explain to their parents how to figure the area on the mixed number problem using the area model. Parents can explain how they would figure this floor's area, and students can report these explanations to the class.

Hints and Comments

Overview

Students read the Summary, which reviews the units of measure that are used in the metric system and the customary system for length and area. It also shows how a drawing can be used when finding area of a floor that does not have whole numbers as side lengths.

Planning

Read and discuss the Summary as a class. Ask students to suggest other units of measurement. You may also want to discuss these common abbreviations:

- cm^2 is square centimeters
- m^2 is square meters
- km^2 is square kilometers
- yd^2 is square yards

To determine whether or not students understand which units are appropriate for measuring various objects, ask the following:

- *What units are useful for measuring the length of a pencil?* (cm, mm, in.) Students' answers will show their understanding of the relationship between the size of the unit that is chosen and the precision of the measurement. You may point out that a millimeter is one-tenth of a centimeter.

- *Why is a meter or a kilometer not suitable for measuring a pencil?* (They are too large.)

- *What unit is suitable for measuring the distance from home to school?* (kilometer or mile)

◆ Measuring Area

Notes

1a This problem revisits area as "filling a space" and creating a tessellation with no gaps or overlaps.

Students may be able see a parallel between how the triangular tiles make hexagons and the way square centimeters make a square meter. Square centimeters are a refinement of the square meter; the triangular tiles are a refinement of the hexagons.

Students may see a repeated pattern in the walkway and not have to divide the whole floor into tiles. Encourage students to use methods other than counting the individual tiles on the walkway.

1b Use the term *equilateral triangle* to describe the small triangular tiles.

Check Your Work

Here is the plan for the main walkway in a new mall. The tiles used to make this floor are in the shape of a hexagon, a six-sided shape.

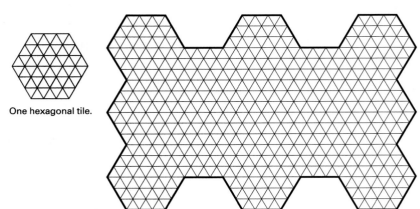

One hexagonal tile.

Main Walkway

1. Use the drawing of the Main Walkway on **Student Activity Sheet 12** to answer the following questions.

    a. How many hexagonal tiles were used to create this walkway?

The hexagonal tiles were made in the factory from small triangular tiles.

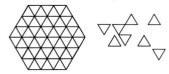

    b. How many of these small triangular tiles are in the floor of the Main Walkway?

Assessment Pyramid

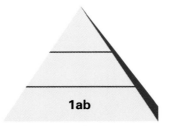

1ab

Assesses Section C Goals

Reaching All Learners

Accommodation

Cut out a model of the hexagonal tile to figure the area of the floor.

Intervention

Pattern blocks (triangles and hexagons) could be used to model and find the walkway area.

Solutions and Samples

Answers to Check Your Work

1. **a.** You need 13 of these tiles.

   b. For the floor of the main walkway, 702 small tiles are needed. In a hexagonal tile, you can see six triangles, each with 9 small tiles. So a hexagonal tile holds $6 \times 9 = 54$ small tiles. The whole walkway is $13 \times 54 = 702$ small tiles.

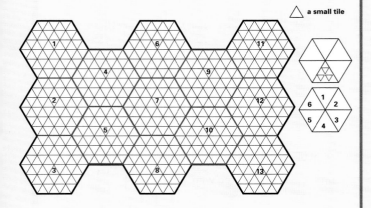

a small tile

Hints and Comments

Overview

Students use the Check Your Work problems as self-assessment. The answers to these problems are also provided on Student Book pages 72 and 73.

Notes

4 Be sure students estimate the area of a surface and not confuse this concept with finding the volume. This question will help you determine if students understand which units are appropriate for measuring areas.

5 Order the customary and metric units separately and then combine them. Refer to the samples students created earlier in this section as references.

Ask, *How do you determine which measurement should be used to find a length or an area?*

Measuring Area

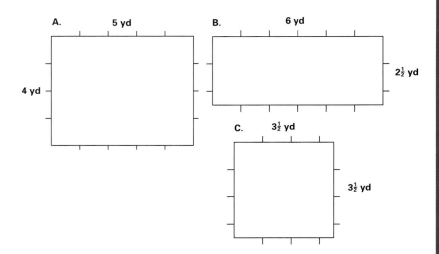

2. Calculate the area (in square yards) of each floor.

3. The floors in problem 2 are covered with colored tiles. Each tile has side lengths of one foot.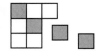

   a. How many tiles do you need to cover each of the floors?

   b. Finish this sentence: 1 square yard = _____ square feet.

4. Name an object and estimate its area using at least two of the measurement units listed in the Summary.

5. Order all the metric and customary units from the Summary in one list from smallest to largest.

 For Further Reflection

Name at least three situations in your house for which it was important to find area.

Assessment Pyramid

☐ FFR

2, 3, 4, 5

Assesses Section C Goals

Reaching All Learners

Accommodation

For problem 4, give the students objects and ask them to tell which measurement unit is most appropriate.

Intervention

Provide a matching exercise for problem 4, with areas and objects, to see if students can choose the best matches.

Use the real-life examples of measurements in problem 5 to order the customary and metric units.

Solutions and Samples

2. A. The area is $4 \times 5 = 20$ square yards. You may either use the formula *area* $= b \times h$, or divide the floor into pieces of 1 yard by 1 yard.

B. The area is $2\frac{1}{2} \times 6 = 15$ square yards. You may either use the formula *area* $= b \times h$, or divide the floor into pieces like the drawing below and calculate the number of squares.

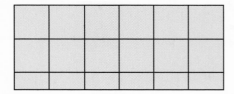

C. The area is $3\frac{1}{2} \times 3\frac{1}{2} = 12\frac{1}{4}\,yd^2$. You may use either one of the strategies used for **B**.

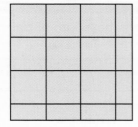

3. a. One yard is 3 feet, so $1\,yd^2$ is $9\,ft^2$. You may want to make a drawing to see why this is the case.

So floor **A** needs $20 \times 9 = 180$ tiles, or you could reason that the dimensions are 15 ft by 12 ft, which would be $15 \times 12 = 180$ tiles.

Floor **B** needs $15 \times 9 = 135$ tiles, or $18 \times 7\frac{1}{2} = 135$ tiles.

Floor **C** needs $12\frac{1}{4} \times 9 = 110\frac{1}{4}$ tiles, or $10\frac{1}{2} \times 10\frac{1}{2} = 110\frac{1}{4}$ tiles

b. $1\,yd^2 = 9\,ft^2$

4. Answers will vary. Some responses you might have are:
- A fingernail is about $1\,cm^2$ or about $100\,mm^2$.
- A poster is about $1\,m^2$ or about $9\,ft^2$.
- A seat cushion is about $1\,ft^2$ or $144\,in^2$.
- Lake Tahoe is about $200\,mi^2$ or $518\,km^2$.

5. Measures listed in order: 1 cm, 1 in., 1 ft, 1 yd, 1 m, 1 km, 1 mi.

Hints and Comments

Overview

Students continue to use the Check Your Work problems as self-assessment. The answers to these problems are also provided on Student Book pages 72 and 73.

Planning

After students complete Section C, you may assign as homework appropriate activities from the Additional Practice section, located on Student Book page 66.

For Further Reflection

Answers may vary. Sample response:

It is important to find the area of part of a house when you need to tile a bathroom floor, carpet rooms, paint walls, tile a terrace, or plant a lawn.

Section Focus

The instructional focus of Section D is to:

- develop students' understanding of the concept of perimeter;
- develop students' understanding of which units and tools are appropriate to estimate and measure perimeter and area; and
- further develop students' formal vocabulary related to shapes, using words like *perimeter, diameter, radius,* and *circumference,* and names like *equilateral triangle* and *regular hexagon.*

Pacing and Planning

Day 12: Perimeter		Student pages 37 and 38
INTRODUCTION	Problem 1	Compare the length of trails around two lakes.
CLASSWORK	Problems 2–4	Measure and compare area and perimeter.
HOMEWORK	Problem 5	Investigate the effect of enlargement on area and perimeter.

Day 13: Areas and Perimeter Enlarged (Continued)		Student pages 39–41
INTRODUCTION	Problem 6	Measure the dimensions of enlarged pictures.
CLASSWORK	Problems 7 and 8	Determine and compare the dimensions of enlarged pictures.
ACTIVITY	Activity, page 40 Problems 9 and 10	Use a string and a pencil to draw a circle and estimate the circumference of a circle.
HOMEWORK	Problems 11 and 12	Use the perimeter of a hexagon and a square to estimate the circumference of a circle.

Day 14: Circles (Continued)		Student pages 42–44
INTRODUCTION	Review homework.	Review homework from Day 13.
CLASSWORK	Problems 13–17	Explain the relationship between the circumference of a circle and its radius.
HOMEWORK	Problem 18	Investigate how an L-shaped terrace may be realloted into a circle-shaped terrace.

Day 15. Circles and Area (Continued)		Student pages 44–48
INTRODUCTION	Review homework.	Review homework from Day 14.
CLASSWORK	Problems 19–22	Apply formulas for finding the area and circumference of circles to solve problems.
HOMEWORK	Check Your Work	Student self-assessment: Solve problems involving area and perimeter.

Day 16. Summary		Student page 48
INTRODUCTION	Review homework.	Review homework from Day 15.
ASSESSMENT	Quiz 2	Assessment of Sections C and D Goals
HOMEWORK	For Further Reflection	Review terms and formulas related to area and perimeter.

Additional Resources: Additional Practice, Section D, Student Book page 67

Materials

Student Resources

Quantities listed are per student.

- **Student Activity Sheets 13** and **14**

Teachers Resources

No resources required

Student Materials

Quantities listed are per student, unless otherwise noted.

- Calculator
- Centimeter ruler
- Compass
- Graph paper (two sheets)
- Scissors
- String—between 20 cm and 30 cm long

* See Hints and Comments for optional materials.

Learning Lines

Area and Perimeter

Just as activities like covering floors with carpet help to develop students' understanding of the concept of area, measuring trails around lakes or fences around gardens helps to develop students' understanding of the concept of perimeter. In this section, students explore relationships between perimeter and area. They discover that:

- two shapes with the same perimeter can have different areas;
- two shapes with the same area can have different perimeters; and
- when a shape is enlarged, the area will enlarge more than the dimensions, or perimeter.

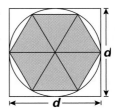

This relationship can be written formally as: *If the factor of enlargement is k, then the factor of enlargement of the area is k^2*. Factors of enlargement and reduction are made explicit in the unit *Ratios and Rates*.

At the End of This Section: Learning Outcomes

Students are able to estimate and calculate the perimeter of a shape and its enlargement. They understand the effect of enlarging a shape. Students have used both informal as well as formal ways to find perimeters. Students can use formulas to compute the circumference and area of a circle.

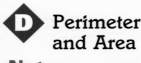
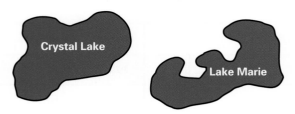

Perimeter and Area

Perimeter

Danny is a contractor hired to build a bicycle/running trail around each of the lakes pictured below. The owner wants to pay Danny the same amount of money for each trail because the lakes are equal in area. Danny agrees that the lakes are equal in area, but he wants more money for constructing the trail around Lake Marie.

1 Students should see that the lake areas are identical, but the perimeters are different.

1. Do you agree that Danny should get more money for the Lake Marie trail? Why or why not?

Here are drawings of four gardens the city wants to plant in a downtown park. Along the outside edge of each garden, the city will build an ornamental fence. Each square in the grid represents 10 m by 10 m.

2 Call students' attention to the fact that the gardens are labeled B through E and that A shows the scale of the grid.

Students will find that these gardens have identical perimeters but that their areas are different. Help students to recognize that this situation is the inverse of problem 1.

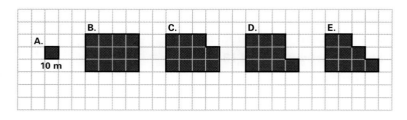

2. How much fencing do you need to fence in each garden?

Reaching All Learners

Extension

Have students estimate what Danny should be paid for the two lake trails. They support their answer with math.

Hands-On Learning

Use string to find the trail lengths. When you extend the strings, the trail lengths can be compared. The string can also be used to confirm that the perimeters of the gardens are the same.

Solutions and Samples

1. Yes, Danny should get more money for the Lake Marie trail because Lake Marie has a larger perimeter.
2. Gardens B–E will need 140 meters of fencing.

Hints and Comments

Materials

string—between 20 and 30 cm long, optional (one per student)

Overview

Students compare the length of a trail around one lake to the length of a trail around another lake. They then measure and compare the perimeters and areas of different-shaped gardens drawn on graph paper.

About the Mathematics

The contexts of trails and fences help students focus on the concept of perimeter as a distance or length around a shape. In problems 3 and 4 on the next page, students discover that figures with identical perimeters can have different areas and that figures with identical areas can have different perimeters.

Planning

You may wish to complete problems 1 and 2 as a whole class or have students work in small groups on these problems and discuss their answers briefly.

Comments About the Solutions

1. and 2.
   Students may use a piece of string to verify their answers.

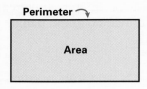

Perimeter and Area

Notes

3a Create a visual representation of area (space inside a polygon) and perimeter (distance around the outside).

Perimeter

Area

3b Be sure students use the correct label for area.

4 This makes a great homework activity.

5 Consider reproducing this enlargement problem for students or providing a transparency since they will want to write on this page.

3. The distance around a shape is called the **perimeter** of the shape.

   a. How is the area of a shape different from its perimeter?

   b. Find the area of each garden.

   c. Compare the area and perimeter of these gardens.

Here is a drawing of a garden with an area of 15 square units.

4. Use graph paper to design four other gardens with the same area but with different perimeters. Label the area and perimeter of each garden.

Area and Perimeter Enlarged

Here are three pairs of figures. For each pair, **Figure i** is enlarged to make **Figure ii**. Each pair has the same shape but not the same size.

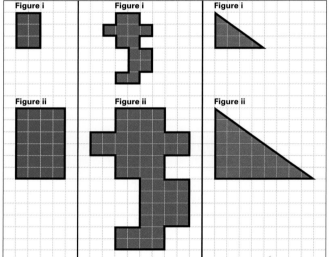

5. For each pair, calculate and compare the area and perimeter of **Figure i** and **Figure ii**. Describe how the area and perimeter are changed if you enlarge a shape by a certain factor.

Assessment Pyramid

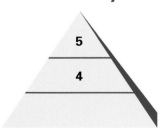

Analyze the effect of change in dimensions.

Solve perimeter and area problems.

Reaching All Learners

Vocabulary Building

Have students add *perimeter* to the vocabulary section of their notebook. Point out that the word *rim* is in the word *perimeter*. This can help students remember that perimeter means around the outside just as the rim means around the outside.

Extension

Ask students to choose the smaller figure from one of the three pairs on Student Book page 38 and enlarge it by making the sides three times longer. Then ask students to investigate the effect of this enlargement on the figure's area and perimeter. (The area will be nine times that of figure **i**. The perimeter will be three times that of figure **i**.)

Solutions and Samples

3. a. Sample response:
The area is how many units cover the shape. The perimeter is how long it is around the shape.

b. B. 12 square meters

C. 11 square meters

D. 10 square meters

E. 9 square meters

c. Answers will vary. Sample response:

The perimeter of each garden is 14 units, but the areas decrease by one square unit as you move from left to right.

4. Drawings will vary. Sample response:

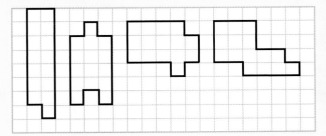

5. In each pair of figures, each side of Figure i has been doubled to get Figure ii. The area of Figure ii is four times that of Figure i. The perimeter of Figure ii is twice that of Figure i.

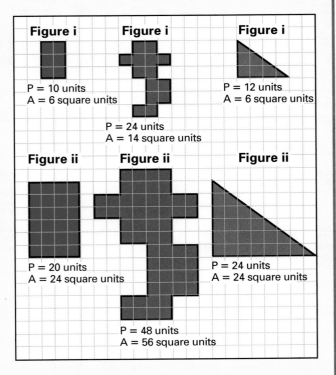

Hints and Comments

Materials

graph paper (one or two sheets per student); transparency of graph paper, optional (one sheet per class)

Overview

Students compare the perimeter and area of a figure with those of its enlargement.

About the Mathematics

Problem 5 helps students understand that area and perimeter are not directly proportional. For example, consider the ratio relationships between these figures shown in the ratio table below.

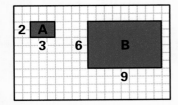

	Height	Base	
Shape A	2	3	1
Shape B	6	9	3

Also consider the ratio relationship between two sides of the first figure and the two corresponding sides of the second figure.

	Shape A	Shape B	
Height	2	6	2
Base	3	9	3

If the corresponding sides of a figure and its enlargement do not have the same ratio, the original figure has been distorted. Enlargements and reductions will be more formally investigated in the unit *Ratios and Rates*.

Comments About the Solutions

3. b. You may have to remind students to use the drawings of the gardens on Student Book page 37.

4. Suggest that students use one side of a grid square as a measuring unit. Some students will incorrectly include a specific unit of measure in their answer. Point out that the grids have no specific unit of measure.

When discussing this problem, you may compare students' results and look for the gardens that have the smallest and largest perimeter.

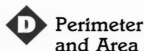

Perimeter and Area

Notes

Show examples of computer created drawings that are enlarged. This effect can be shown when you pull on the corner handlebars of a piece of clipart/graphic on the computer. If you pull the corner handlebar, the graphic enlarges proportionally. Pulling on a handlebar in the middle of a side will change the proportion so that only the length or width is enlarged and the picture becomes distorted. This could lead to a discussion of how to double the area.

Here is an original picture of space ships (Picture **A**).

6. Use a centimeter ruler to measure the dimensions of the picture.

This picture can be enlarged. Different enlargements of the same picture have the same shape but not the same dimensions.

Here is an enlargement (Picture **B**) of the original picture. It was enlarged from the original by a factor of two. This means that both the length and width were doubled.

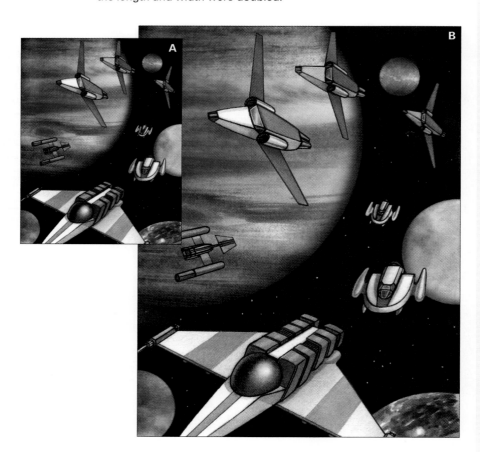

Reaching All Learners

Extension

Have students create multiple enlargements of a graphic. They can print the original and the enlargements, compare the dimensions and areas on a chart, and share results with the class.

Solutions and Samples

6. Length = 8 cm, width = 6 cm.

Hints and Comments

Materials

centimeter rulers (one per student);
overhead projector, optional (one per class);
transparency of the two rectangles on this page, optional (one per class)

Overview

Students measure the dimensions of a picture, and they start to investigate an enlargement of a picture.

Planning

You may assign problem 6 for homework and discuss it the next day in class. Focus on the relationships between the measurements and on the fact that the pictures have the same shape. Almost all students will notice that a shape changes when a rectangle's height is enlarged by more than its width. However, some students may say that the shape remains the same because it is still a rectangle. To clear up this misconception, you might use the chalkboard or make a transparency of the rectangles below. Ask students whether Figure A could be enlarged to produce Figure B.

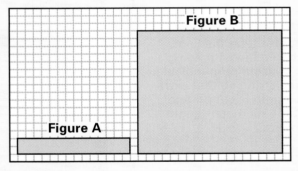

This discussion will prepare students for problems 7 and 8 on the next page.

Comments About the Solutions

6. Students' answers may vary, depending upon their ability to make precise measurements. Accept answers within two millimeters of the answers given in the Solutions column.

◆ Perimeter and Area

Notes

7a If students use picture A to cover picture B, they will see that four times as much glass is required.

The price of glass depends on the area of the picture, and the price of the frame depends on the perimeter of the picture.

When the perimeter doubles (x2), the area quadruples (x4).

8 When the perimeter is tripled, the area is nine times larger.

Activity

Model cutting the knot. It should be cut holding the scissors perpendicular to the string so that extra tail length is cut off and just the diameter length remains.

To frame the original picture (A), a piece of glass costs $5, and a wood frame of 28 cm costs $10.

7. a. If the cost is the same per square centimeter of area for the glass, what is the cost to cover the enlargement (picture B) with glass?

    b. If the cost is the same per centimeter of length for the frame, what is the cost of a wood frame for the enlargement?

Suppose the original print was enlarged to 18 cm by 24 cm.

8. a. What is the cost to cover this enlargement with glass?

    b. What is the cost to border this enlargement with a wood frame?

    c. When a figure is enlarged, will the area and perimeter enlarge in the same way? Explain your answer.

Circumference

The perimeter of shapes that have straight sides can be measured or calculated rather easily. Shapes with curved edges make it more challenging to find the perimeter.

Activity

Drawing a Circle

- Take a string of a length between 20 cm and 30 cm.
- Fold it and knot the ends together.
- Hold the knot in one spot on your paper.
- Put a pencil through the loop at the other end.
- Keeping the rope tight, draw a circle.
- Use scissors to cut through the knot.

Assessment Pyramid

7, 8

Understand the relationship between the perimeter and area of a shape and its enlargement.

Reaching All Learners

Accommodation

Draw the original picture and the enlarged picture on graph paper to help students visualize the changes in area and perimeter. Model the Activity on the board.

Extension

Have students create other problems where the area quadruples when the perimeter doubles. They figure out how the area could double. *What would change in the perimeter?*

Advanced Learners

Have students investigate what happens to the area when the perimeter is cut in half (area is $\frac{1}{4}$ the original size) and report these findings. *What happens to the glass and frame costs?*

Solutions and Samples

7. a. The glass will now cost 4 × 5 = $20, since the glass covers the area, and the area is 4 times as large.

b The frame will cost 2 × 10 = $20. The frame can be seen as being the perimeter. The perimeter of the enlargement is twice the perimeter of the original since all sides have been doubled in length, so the price must be doubled too.

8. a. The glass will cost 9 × $5 = $45. Different strategies can lead to this answer.

- Students may make a drawing to see how many times the original picture fits into the enlarged picture; this is 9 times, so the glass will be 9 times as expensive.

- Another strategy uses area more explicitly. The glass covers the area of the print, so 6 × 8 = 48 cm² costs $5. The area of the enlarged picture is 18 × 24 = 432 cm².

  This is 9 × 48, so it will cost 9 × $5, which is $45.

b. The frame will cost $30. Different strategies can lead to this answer.

- Students can use what they learned in problems 6 and 7. The original picture is 6 cm by 8 cm. The enlarged picture has sides 3 times as long.

- Students may make a drawing and conclude that the perimeter is also three times as long, so the frame is 3 times as expensive.

- Another strategy uses perimeter more explicitly: the frame can be seen as perimeter. The perimeter of the original picture is 8 + 6 + 8 + 6 = 28 cm, and 28 cm costs $10. The perimeter of the enlarged picture is: 24 + 18 + 24 + 18 = 84 cm. This is 3 × 28 so will cost 3 × $10, which is $30.

c. In problem 7, the picture was enlarged two times. The perimeter was also enlarged two times, but the area was enlarged four times. In problem 8, the picture and its perimeter were enlarged three times, but the area was enlarged nine times.

Hints and Comments

Materials

string—between 20 cm and 30 cm long (one per student);
scissors (one pair per student)

Overview

Students calculate the cost of framing enlargements of the picture with glass and a wood frame. They reflect on whether or not the area and perimeter of an enlargement change in the same way.

Students use a string and a pencil to draw a circle.

Planning

You may have students work on problems 7 and 8 individually and use these problems as informal assessment. Students may work individually or in pairs on the activity.

Comments About the Solutions

8. The price of the glass depends on the area of the picture, and the price of the frame depends on the perimeter of the picture. Some students may draw the enlarged picture to help them see the difference in the bases of the price for the glass and the price for the frame.

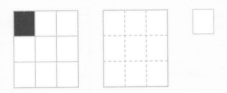

Activity

When students finish the activity, you may demonstrate it on the board, using a piece of chalk and string or a shoelace. This drawing can be used when discussing students' responses to problem 9 on the next page. Note that students need to use their drawing and the string for problem 9 on the next page.

D Perimeter and Area

Notes

Discuss the relationship between perimeter (distance around the outside of a polygon) and circumference (distance around the outside of a circle).

11 Students should estimate that the perimeter of the circle (circumference) is less than the perimeter of the square and greater than the perimeter of the hexagon.

Use a transparency of the square that encloses the circle and hexagon to show that you can figure the perimeter of the square by comparing the square's side length to the circle's diameter. Then each side of the square is 2 cm.

9. a. What is the special name given to the length of the string?

b. About how many times does the length of the string fit along the perimeter of the circle?

c. Compare your answer to part **b** with your classmates'.

Circles

A more precise method to find the perimeter of a circle would be very useful.

First you need an **equilateral triangle**.

Equilateral means that all sides have the same length.

Using six of these regular triangles, you can make a **regular hexagon**.

10. a. What is the perimeter of the regular triangle?

b. What is the perimeter of the regular hexagon?

Here is an enlargement of this hexagon.

A circle is drawn around the hexagon. The circle passes through all six corners.

A square is drawn to enclose both the circle and hexagon.

11. Use the drawings to estimate the perimeter of this circle. Show your work.

The perimeter of a circle is usually called the **circumference** of a circle.

The straight line through the center of the circle is called the **diameter** of the circle.

12. What is the length of the diameter of the circle in problem 11?

Reaching All Learners

Vocabulary Building

Have students note relationships between *equilateral triangles* and *regular hexagons* (same side lengths) and between *diameter* and *circumference* (diameter is used to find the circumference) in the vocabulary section of the student notebook.

Advanced Learners

Have students investigate this diameter-to-circumference relationship with a variety of circles. Ask, *What do you notice when you compare the length of the diameter to that particular circle's circumference?*

Solutions and Samples

9. a. It is the diameter.

 b. The string will fit a little more than 3 times along the perimeter of the circle.

 c. All students should have an answer close to 3 times around.

10. a. 3 cm

 b. 6 cm

11. The perimeter will be a little more than 6 cm, which is the perimeter of the hexagon inside. The perimeter is certainly less than 8 cm, which is the perimeter of the square around the circle.

12. The diameter is 2 cm.
Note that some students might try to measure this. If they do, they will find it is more like 2.5 cm.

The diameter in the enlargement is 3.2 cm.

Hints and Comments

Materials

transparency of page 41, optional

Overview

Students investigate how many times the length of their string fit along the perimeter of the circle. Students are introduced to the concept of the circumference of a circle and they estimate the circumference of a circle using the perimeter of a hexagon that fits just inside the circle and a square that just fits around the circle.

About the Mathematics

The drawing below shows that the estimated circumference of the circle is between the perimeter of the hexagon and the perimeter of the square. The perimeters of the shapes can be expressed in a more formal way using the diameter (d) of the circle. The perimeter of the square is $4 \times d$ and the perimeter of the hexagon is $3 \times d$. The picture shows that the circumference of the circle is closer to $3 \times d$ than $4 \times d$.

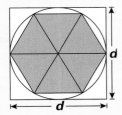

Planning

Students may work on problem 9 individually or in pairs. Then you might want to discuss the terms *diameter*, *radius*, and *hexagon* before students begin problem 10. Students can work in pairs or in small groups on problems 10–12.

Comments About the Solutions

 9. Students should see that the string fits a little more than three times around the circle, independently of the length of the string.

D Perimeter and Area

Notes

Here are three new drawings made using different sizes of equilateral triangles. The triangle size is shown in each drawing.

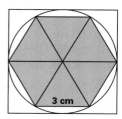

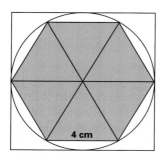

13. Use the figures above to calculate the perimeter of each square and hexagon. Use the diameter of each circle to estimate the circumferences of each circle. Write all the results in the table on **Student Activity Sheet 13**.

	Estimating the Circumference			
	Using 1-cm Triangles	**Using 2-cm Triangles**	**Using 3-cm Triangles**	**Using 4-cm Triangles**
Diameter of Circle				
Perimeter of Hexagon				
Approximate Circumference of Circle				
Perimeter of Square				

Review the results in your table.

14. **a.** How is the circumference of each circle related to the perimeter of the hexagon and the square that belongs to it?

b. Describe the relationship between the diameter of a circle and its circumference.

c. Compare this result to your findings from problem 9.

14a The calculation should show that the circumference of the circles would fall between the perimeters of the hexagon and the square, but closer to the hexagon.

14b The circumference should be a little more than three times the diameter in each case.

Reaching All Learners

Hands-On Learning

Have students create another chart, locate circles of various sizes, measure their diameters, and estimate their circumferences. They use string to check the estimates. Then they can produce a statement about how to find the circumference of any circle.

Advanced Learners

Have students figure out a formula for showing how to get π (pi) if you know the circumference and the diameter.

Solutions and Samples

13.

	Estimating the Circumference			
	Using 1-cm Triangles	Using 2-cm Triangles	Using 3-cm Triangles	Using 4-cm Triangles
Diameter of Circle	2 cm	4 cm	6 cm	8 cm
Perimeter of Hexagon	6 cm	12 cm	18 cm	24 cm
Approximate Circumference of Circle	a little more than 6 cm	a little more than 12 cm	a little more than 18 cm	a little more than 24 cm
Perimeter of Square	8 cm	16 cm	24 cm	32 cm

14. a. Answers will vary. Sample response:

The perimeter of the circle is a little bit larger than the perimeter of the hexagon, but it's smaller than the perimeter of the square. The perimeter of the circle is a little more than $\frac{3}{4}$ of the perimeter of the square.

b. The circumference of a circle is a little more than 3 times the diameter.

c. This is about the same result that was found for problem 9.

Hints and Comments

Materials

Student Activity Sheet 13 (one per student)

Overview

Students investigate regular hexagons of different sizes that are enclosed within a circle and a square. They then investigate the perimeters of these shapes.

Planning

Students can work in pairs or in small groups on problems 13 and 14. Check students' answers to problem 13 and discuss their responses to problem 14.

Comments About the Solutions

13. The perimeters of the squares and the hexagons can be found without measuring. Students have to use the side lengths that are indicated in the drawings.

Again, students should estimate that the perimeter of the circle is less than the perimeter of the square and greater than the perimeter of the hexagon.

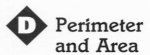

Perimeter and Area

Notes

Access calculators and convert $\frac{22}{7}$ into a decimal. Find the π symbol on the calculator and discuss as a class why it is ≈ 3.14.

Ask students, *If C is the circumference of a circle, what will be the result of C ÷ d?*

17 Use a metric ruler to draw a 6-cm line segment horizontally and vertically that crosses at the 3 cm mark in both directions and then try to form the circle around these two diameter distances.

We use an uppercase "C" to represent circumference and a lowercase "d" and "r" for diameter and radius, respectively.

Long ago, people discovered a relationship between the circumference of a circle and the diameter of the circle. They described this relationship like this.

"The *circumference of circle* is a FIXED NUMBER times the *diameter of circle*."

15. What is the value of this fixed number based on your findings so far?

The ancient Greeks used a special name for this fixed number. They called it **π** (a letter in the Greek alphabet, pronounced PYE). Pi is approximately 3.14 or $\frac{22}{7}$.

A rough estimate for the value of pi is the number 3.

The modern formula for the circumference of circle is:

circumference of circle = π × *diameter of circle*

Using an approximation for **π**, the formula becomes:

circumference of circle $\approx$ 3.14 × *diameter of circle*

Most calculators today have a **π** button for this special fixed number.

16. a. What value does your calculator display for the number **π**?

    b. Use one of the formulas above to check your circumference estimates for the circles recorded in your table in problem 13.

Some people prefer to use the **radius** of a circle when they find the circumference of a circle.

The radius of a circle is half the size of the diameter.

17. a. Draw a circle with a diameter of 6 cm in your notebook. Color the radius of the circle and write its length next to the drawing. Find the circumference of the circle.

    b. Use your drawing to explain this formula:

circumference of circle = 2 × **π** × *radius of circle*

Reaching All Learners

Vocabulary Building

Radius can be added to the vocabulary section of the student notebook with an illustration and the formulas for finding circumference.

Advanced Learners

π actually stands for a very interesting decimal number. Have students find the decimal to 25 (or more) places and look for patterns, investigate how π was discovered and by whom, and display their findings in the classroom.

Extension

Many math classes celebrate π Day (Pi Day). Ask, *When should this celebration take place, why did you pick this date, and how could you celebrate?*

Solutions and Samples

15. This fixed number is a little more than 3.

16. a. The π key will generate a number
3.141592654…

b. The formulas give the following results for calculated circumferences.

First column: 2π or 6.28 cm

Second column: 4π or 12.56 cm

Third column: 6π or 18.85 cm

Fourth column: 8π or 25.12 cm

17 a. Sample drawing:

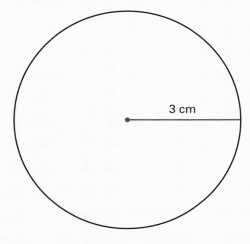

3 cm

The circumference of this circle is
6 × π ≈ 18.85 cm.

b. Sample explanations:

- The circumference of a circle is π × diameter, and the diameter is 2 × radius, so the circumference is π × 2 × radius, which is the same as 2 × π × radius.

- The diameter fits a little more than three times, or π times, around its circle. Since the radius is just half of the diameter, the radius will fit a little more than six times around its circle, which is 2 × π.

Hints and Comments

Materials

calculators (one per student);
compasses (one per student);
centimeter rulers (one per student)

Overview

Students investigate different ways to describe the relationship between the circumference of a circle and its diameter. They are introduced to the number π. Students explain the relationship between the circumference of a circle and its radius.

About the Mathematics

In a circle, the ratio of the circumference to the diameter is constant. Students can discover this ratio by dividing a circle's circumference by its diameter to get a number a little greater than 3. This ratio $\frac{C}{d}$ is commonly referred to as π.

Planning

You may want to read the text and complete problem 15 as a class. Ask students to explain their answers to problem 15. When they say the circumference is something between 3 and 4 times the diameter, you can ask them, *Will it be between 3 and 3.5 times or between 3.5 and 4 times?* (Between 3 and 3.5 times.)

Then discuss the number π and the common estimates that are used for π (see also the Math History on Student Book page 59). Students may work on problems 16 and 17 individually or in small groups.

Comments About the Solutions

17. a. Some students may not have much experience in drawing circles using a compass. If you see a student struggling, you may give some hints on how to use this tool.

Note that some students may draw a circle with a radius of 6 cm.

To calculate the circumference, students may use a calculator and the π key, or 3.14 as an estimate for π.

When discussing students' answers, you may introduce the ≈ sign that can be used to indicate that the answer is an estimate or rounded.

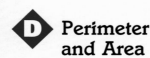
Notes

18a Students can use a transparency to explain their methods for finding the number of tiles.

The answers to 18a and 18b are similar. Students may be able to see how the "corners" of the square could be reallotted in the empty $\frac{1}{4}$ of the circle and thus fill the rest of the circle's area.

Compare the formulas for circumference and area of a circle. Discuss the difference between $C = 2\pi r$ and $A = \pi r^2$.

19a Note that the area enclosed by the circle is about $\frac{3}{4}$ of the area of the square that just fits around it.

Circles and Area

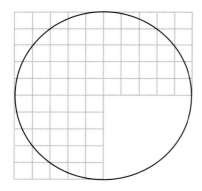

Peter's mother has an L-shaped terrace. She would like to change this L-shaped terrace into a circle shape. Here is a drawing to represent her design.

18. a. How many tiles are in the L-shaped terrace? Use **Student Activity Sheet 14** to help you answer the question. Explain how you found your answer.

b. Estimate the number of tiles needed to create the circle-shaped terrace.

An ancient formula used to estimate the area enclosed by a circle is: the *area* is about 3 × *radius* × *radius*.

19. a. Use the small drawing above and the drawing for problem 18 on **Student Activity Sheet 14** to explain why this ancient formula is a good estimate for the area enclosed by a circle.

b. Use this ancient formula to check your answer to problem 18b.

A more precise number you can use instead of 3 is surprisingly the number π!

A modern formula for the area enclosed by a circle is:

$$area\ enclosed\ by\ a\ circle = \pi \times radius \times radius$$

or, $$area \approx 3.14 \times radius \times radius$$

The square tiles in problem 18 are 30 cm by 30 cm.

20. a. Calculate the area of the circle-shaped terrace using one of the formulas above.

b. Compare this result to your estimates for 18b and 19b.

Assessment Pyramid

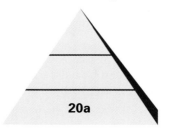

Use formulas for finding the area enclosed by a circle.

Reaching All Learners

Vocabulary Building

The *area formula* and an illustration for using it should be added to the student notebook.

Hands-On Learning

For problem 18a, have students reproduce on graph paper or copy the terrace problem and cut off the corners of the square outside of the circle. Then they try to "fit" the pieces into the missing circle fourth to find out if the three corners are approximately equal to that area.

Solutions and Samples

18. a. 75 tiles

Sample explanation: I see three squares. Each square contains 25 tiles. So the total number of tiles is 3 × 25, which is 75.

b. Also about 75 tiles. Students may extend the grid inside the circle and then estimate the total number of squares by smart counting. Another option is to "cut off" the parts outside the circle and fit these in the remaining quarter of the circle.

19. a. The area of the circle is about the area of the three squares (see problem 18). Each square has an area of radius of the circle × radius of the circle. So the area of the circle is 3 × radius × radius.

b. The radius is 5, so the area is about 3 × 5 × 5 = 75 square units or tiles.

20. a. 70,650 square centimeters, or about 7 square meters. Sample calculations:

- Each tile is 30 cm long, so the radius of the circle is 150 cm, and the area is 3.14 × 150 × 150 = 70,650 square centimeters.

- Using meters (which makes more sense), the area is 3.14 × 1.5 × 1.5 = 7.065 square meters, which is about 7 square meters.

b. In problem 18b, there were 75 tiles. One tile has an area of 30 × 30 = 900 square centimeters. 75 tiles cover an area of 75 × 900 = 67,500 square centimeters. This is a little less than the calculation for 20a.

In problem 19b, the formula is 3 × *radius* × *radius*; since the radius is 150 cm, you calculate 3 × 150 × 150, which is 67,500 square centimeters. This is also a little less than the calculation for 20a.

Hints and Comments

Materials
Student Activity Sheet 14 (one per student); calculators (one per student)

Overview

Students investigate how an L-shaped terrace may be realloted into a circle-shaped terrace. In this way, students start to investigate the area enclosed by a circle. They use different given formulas to find areas enclosed by circles.

Planning

You may have students work on problems 18–20 in small groups. Discuss students' responses to problems 18 and 19 and the text after problem 19 before they continue with problem 20. To see each individual student's understanding of using formulas for finding the area enclosed by a circle, you might use problem 20a as informal assessment.

Comments About the Solutions

18. When discussing this problem, you may look back to problem 14a. The perimeter of the circle is a little more than $\frac{3}{4}$ of the perimeter of the square. In problem 18, a similar relationship can be found; the area enclosed by the circle is a little more than $\frac{3}{4}$ of the area enclosed by the square.

Extension

A different way to find a formula for the area enclosed by a circle is the following:

Cut a circle in sections and transform the circle into a parallelogram: You may demonstrate this transformation by cutting apart the segments of a circle and rearranging them on an overhead projector to form a parallelogram.

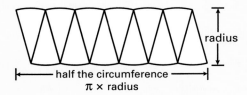

Perimeter and Area

Notes

Note that the glass is sold by the square foot and the oak trim by the linear foot, terms you may need to discuss with students. The window measurements are in inches. Students may want to change the window dimensions into feet to do this problem, OR convert the final answer of sq in. into sq ft. One sq ft equals 144 sq in.

The formulas for area and perimeters related to circles have many practical uses. Here are the designs for two mirrors, one a circle and the other a rectangle with a semicircle on top.

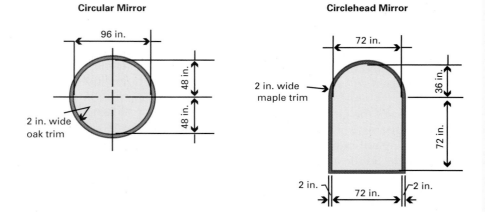

Circular Mirror

96 in.

48 in.

48 in.

2 in. wide oak trim

Circlehead Mirror

72 in.

2 in. wide maple trim

36 in.

72 in.

2 in.

72 in.

2 in.

21. Tamae was going to buy the largest mirror she could find.

   a. Which of the two mirrors has the larger viewing area? Explain your reasoning.

   b. Which of the two mirrors has the greater perimeter? How do you know?

   c. Which mirror should Tamae buy? Why?

A pizza that is 10 in. in diameter costs $9.60 while a 12-in. pizza costs $11.80. Joni says, "For 2 in. more, I have to pay an extra $2.20."

Alex states, "But you get a lot more pizza if you by the big one."

22. a. Comment on the statements made by Joni and Alex.

   b. How much more pizza is the big one compared to the small one?

Assessment Pyramid

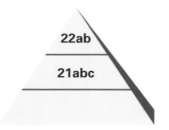

22ab

21abc

Analyze the effect of change in dimension on area.

Solve area and perimeter problems.

Reaching All Learners

Intervention

For problems 21 and 22, have students type the steps to find area and circumference, to convert from one measurement to another, and to find the cost.

Extension

Have students make a list of the different circles in which someone would want to find circumference or area and give the reasons why.

Advanced Learners

Ask, *If you owned the pizza restaurant, what would you charge for a 12-in. pizza if the 10-in. pizza was $9.60?* Tell students to be ready to defend their answer.

Solutions and Samples

21 a. The circular mirror—its area is a little larger than the area of the other mirror.

Sample calculations:

Circular mirror (left)

The radius of the circle is 48 in., which is 4 ft.

Area circle = $\pi \times radius \times radius = \pi \times 4 \times 4 \approx$ 50.24 ft² (or 7,238 square inches).

Circlehead mirror (right)

The sides of the square are 72 in., which is 6 ft.

Area square = $6 \times 6 = 36$ ft² (or 5,184 square inches).

The radius of the half circle is 36 in., which is 3 ft.

Area whole circle = $\pi \times 3 \times 3 \approx 28.3$ ft² (or 4,072 square inches).

So the area of half the circle is about 14.15 ft² (or 2,036 square inches).

Total area is about $36 + 14 = 50$ ft² (or 7220 square inches).

b. The circlehead mirror has a greater perimeter.

Sample calculations:

Circular mirror (left)

The diameter of the circle is 8 ft.

Circumference circle = $8 \times \pi \approx 25.1$ ft.

Circlehead mirror (right)

Perimeter of the bottom part is $3 \times 6 = 18$ ft.

The circumference of a whole circle is $6 \times \pi \approx 18.8$, so the circumference of half this circle is about 9.4 ft.

Total perimeter is 18 ft $+ 9.4$ ft $= 27.4$ ft.

c. Responses and explanations may vary. Sample answer: Tamae should buy the circlehead mirror because its height is 108 in. or 9 ft. It is also better for viewing her total height.

22. a. Sample response:

I think that Alex's statement makes sense, because the area is enlarged more than the diameter. But I have to calculate to see how much more pizza you will get.

Hints and Comments

Overview

Students apply formulas for finding the area and circumference of circles to solve problems.

About the Mathematics

The relationship between the factor of enlargement of the diameter (length) and the factor of enlargement of the area can be written formally as:

If the factor of enlargement is k, then the factor of enlargement of the area is k^2.

A factor of enlargement will be made explicit in the unit *Ratios and Rates*. Do not discuss this with your students unless they come up this relationship by themselves, in which case you may discuss this informally.

Planning

You may have students work on problems 21 and 22 individually or in small groups. You might want to use these problems to informally assess (groups of) students. Discuss these problems in class.

Comments About the Solutions

21. Students may use their understanding of the customary system to convert inches into feet.

Note: It is easier to convert the dimensions first and then find the area in square feet, than first calculate the area in square inches and then convert these into square feet. When students use square inches and square feet in their answers, you may discuss how to compare these different answers. (Note that one square foot equals 144 square inches; see also Student Book page 28, problem 8.)

b. Sample response:

The area of the 10-in. pizza is $\pi \times 5 \times 5 \approx 78.5$ square inches. The area of the 12-in. pizza is $\pi \times 6 \times 6 \approx 113.1$ square inches. So you get 34.6 square inches more pizza, which is almost half the 10-in. pizza. Or you can say that the area of the 12-in. pizza is almost one-and-a-half times larger than the area of the 10-in. pizza. Since the price is less than one and a half times more, it is a good deal.

Perimeter and Area

Notes

Read this Summary aloud. Determine some circles' diameter or radius lengths and find the circumference or area for practice. Use calculators.

Ask students to discuss why we have two formulas for the circumference of a circle. Also be sure that students recognize that $2 \times r\ (2r)$ is NOT equal to $r \times r\ (r^2)$. Use numbers to represent "r," and note the differences between $2r$ and r^2.

Also pictures may be helpful to show the difference:

r^2

$2r$

Summary

In this section, you studied relationships between perimeter and area. You learned that:

- two shapes with the same perimeter can have different areas, and
- two shapes with the same area can have different perimeters.

You investigated what happens to area and perimeter when a figure is enlarged.

When all the lengths of a shape are doubled, the perimeter of the enlargement doubles, but the area will be enlarged by a factor of 4.

You discovered formulas for circles.

- The perimeter or the distance around the circle is the circumference of the circle (C) and

  is equal to π times the diameter (**d**).

  $$C = \pi \times d$$

If you double the radius, you get the length of the diameter. Another formula is:

  The circumference (C) is equal to two times π times the radius (r).

  $$C = 2 \times \pi \times r$$

π is a fixed number. A good approximation is 3.14 or $\frac{22}{7}$. A rough estimate is 3.

- The **area enclosed by a circle**:

  The area (**A**), enclosed by the circle is equal to π times the radius (r) times the radius (r).

  $$A = \pi \times r \times r \quad \text{or} \quad A = \pi \times r^2$$

Reaching All Learners

Vocabulary Building

The illustrations and vocabulary related to circles from this Summary should be added to the vocabulary section of the student notebook: *circumference, diameter, radius, pi,* and *area.*

Extension

Have students give an example of when they might use $\frac{22}{7}$ as π rather than 3.14.

Advanced Learners

Have students investigate what happens to the circumference and area of a circle if the diameter is doubled or cut in half. They report their findings and compare this information to rectangle or polygon enlargements from this section.

Hints and Comments

Overview

Students read the Summary, which reviews the formulas for finding the perimeter and circumference of a circle.

Planning

Students who have had little experience with formulas may need to use word formulas to express the relationships. You may have them write the formulas that are shown in the Summary as word formulas.

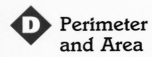

D Perimeter and Area

Notes

Students can work in groups to complete Check Your Work.

They use graph paper and calculators.

4 An insu*rance premium* is the cost of insurance coverage.

---

1. **a.** Draw three different rectangles that enclose an area of 16 cm². What is the perimeter of each rectangle?

   b. What is the smallest perimeter you can have for a rectangle that encloses an area of 16 cm²? Explain your answer.

2. **a.** On graph paper, draw a rectangle that encloses an area of 12 squares. What is its perimeter?

   b. Draw an enlargement of your rectangle by doubling each side.

   c. What is the area enclosed by the enlarged rectangle? What is the perimeter?

   d. In general, if you double all the sides of a rectangle, what happens to the enclosed area? What happens to the perimeter? Explain your answers.

3. Suze wants a clock that is not too large. She is looking at two clocks in the catalog. One has the shape of a circle that is 30 cm in diameter. The other has a rectangular shape (with a clock on it) that is 32 cm by 22 cm.

   Compare the area and the perimeter of each clock. Which one should she buy? Support your answer.

4. Mr. Anderson wants to have glass insurance for his house. The premium for this insurance is based on the area of the exterior glass windows.

   Most of the exterior windows of Mr. Anderson's house have the shape of rectangles.

   a. Describe how Mr. Anderson can calculate the glass area for these windows.

   b. Three windows have the shape shown in the diagram with a semicircle on the top of a rectangle. Describe how Mr. Anderson can calculate the area of glass in this type of window. Include an example of an area calculation for the window with the dimensions in the drawing.

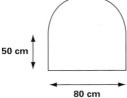

Assessment Pyramid

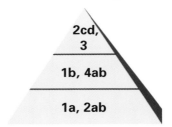

2cd, 3

1b, 4ab

1a, 2ab

Assesses Section D Goals

Reaching All Learners

Intervention

Have students change problem 4 to just a circular window or just a rectangular window.

Extension

Ask, *If problem 1b was a garden and you were going to put a fence around it, what would this mean for your fence length and cost?* (This would be the shortest fence length you would need and therefore the least expensive.)

Parent Involvement

Have students work with their parents to find out if insurance companies provide window insurance and who would need this type of insurance. (Those living near a golf course or airport!)

Solutions and Samples

Answers to Check Your Work

1. a. You can make different drawings. For example:

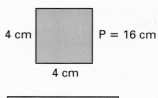

4 cm   P = 16 cm

4 cm

2 cm   P = 20 cm

8 cm

1 cm   P = 34 cm

16 cm

b. The smallest perimeter you can have is the perimeter of the square, which is 16 cm.

2. a. You may have drawn one of the rectangles below.

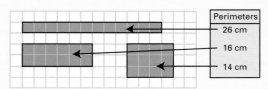

Perimeters
26 cm
16 cm
14 cm

b.

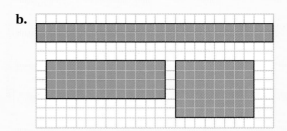

c. The area enclosed by the enlarged rectangle that is 2 by 24 is 48 squares. The perimeter of this rectangle is 52.

The area enclosed by the enlarged rectangle that is 4 by 12 is 48 squares. The perimeter of this rectangle is 32.

The area enclosed by the enlarged rectangle that is 6 by 8 is 48 squares. The perimeter of this rectangle is 28.

d. The area is four times as large since the first rectangle encloses an area of 12 squares, and the enlarged rectangle an area of 48 squares (4 × 12 = 48). If the sides are doubled, the perimeter is doubled.

3. The clocks seem to be about the same size. You are asked to compare the area and the perimeter of the clocks.

Hints and Comments

Overview

Students use the Check Your Work problems as self-assessment. The answers to these problems are also provided on Student Book pages 74–77.

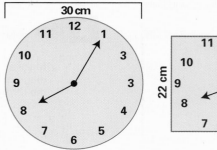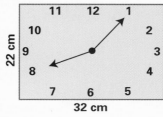

The area of the round clock is $\pi \times r \times r$. The radius r is half of the diameter, or 15 cm.

So the area is $\pi \times 15 \times 15 \approx 707$ cm^2.

The area of the rectangular clock is $b \times h$, which is $32 \times 22 = 704$ cm^2.

So the area of the circular clock is slightly larger.

The perimeter of the round clock is $2 \times \pi \times 15 \approx 94$ cm.

The perimeter of the rectangular clock is $2 \times 32 + 2 \times 22 = 108$ cm.

So the perimeter of the rectangular clock is larger.

Suze will probably use the area to decide which clock is smaller. The rectangular one will take up slightly less area on the wall. If on the other hand, Suze wants to hang the clock in a place that has a maximum height and width of 30 cm, only the round clock will fit.

4. a. Mr. Anderson can calculate the area of glass in the rectangular windows by measuring the height and width of each window, calculating the area by using the rule *area = h × w*, and then adding all the areas.

b. Mr. Anderson can divide the shape of the other window into a rectangular part with half a circle on top.

The area of the rectangular part is *height × width*, which in this case is 50 × 80 = 4,000 cm^2.

The area of the half circle is $0.5 \times \pi \times r \times r$, which in this case is $0.5 \times \pi \times 40 \times 40 \approx$ 2,513 cm^2.

So the glass area of this window is 4,000 + 2,513 or about 6,513 cm^2.

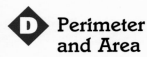

Notes

5 Students can draw this change on graph paper.

 D Perimeter and Area

5. a. What happens to the circumference of a circle if you double the length of the diameter? Justify your answer.

b. What happens to the area enclosed by a circle if you multiply the diameter by 2? Justify your answer.

For Further Reflection

Make a list of all of the terms and formulas in this section. Create a diagram that shows how the terms are related to each other and to the formulas.

Assessment Pyramid

5ab

☐FFR

Assesses Section D Goals

Reaching All Learners

Extension

Problem 5b could represent two pizzas of different sizes or areas. Ask, *How would you price these two pizzas?*

Advanced Learners

Students might contact a pizza restaurant and find out how they price pizzas. Ask, *What is the size and price difference between two different-sized pizzas with the same toppings? Do you think this price difference is reasonable? What is the best deal and why?*

Solutions and Samples

5. a. The circumference is doubled. You might say:

If you double the diameter the circumference also doubles. If the diameter is 10 cm, then the circumference is 3.14 × 10 cm, or 31.40 cm. If the diameter is 20 cm, then the circumference is 3.14 × 20 cm. or 62.80 cm.

b. The area is four times as big, or quadrupled. One explanation you might give is below.

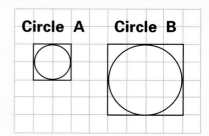

You can draw circles on a grid. Each circle is about $\frac{3}{4}$ of the area enclosed by a square.

The area enclosed by circle A is $\frac{3}{4} \times 2 \times 2 = 3$ square units.

The area enclosed by circle B is $\frac{3}{4} \times 4 \times 4 = 12$ square units, which is four times as big as 3.

Hints and Comments

Materials

graph paper, optional

Overview

Students continue to use the Check Your Work problems as self-assessment. The answers to these problems are also provided on Student Book pages 74–77.

Planning

After students complete Section D, you may assign as homework appropriate activities from the Additional Practice section, located on Student Book page 67.

Section Focus

The instructional focus of Section E is to:

- develop students' understanding of the concept of volume and surface area;
- develop students' understanding of which units and tools are appropriate to estimate and measure volume; and
- further develop students' formal vocabulary related to shapes using terms like *surface area, volume, base,* and *cubic units.*

Pacing and Planning

Day 17: Packages		Student pages 49–52
INTRODUCTION	Problem 1	Compare two packages of modeling clay with respect to the amount of clay and with respect to the amount of wrapping paper.
CLASSWORK	Problems 2–7	Solve problems about packages and numbers of cubes.
HOMEWORK	Problem 8	Find the volume of a package that is partially filled with cubes.

Day 18: Measuring Inside (Continued)		Student pages 53–55
INTRODUCTION	Review homework.	Review homework from Day 17.
CLASSWORK	Problems 10–14	Investigate whether a sack of packing material is enough to fill a package with given dimensions and find relationships between the metric and customary units for volume.
HOMEWORK	Problem 15	Find the volume of different shapes.

Day 19: Reshaping (Continued)		Student pages 56–58
INTRODUCTION	Review homework.	Review homework from Day 18.
CLASSWORK	Problems 16–20	Apply a formula for finding the volume of a shape that can be cut into congruent slices.
HOMEWORK	Problems 21 and 22	Find possible dimensions of a box with a given volume.

Day 20. Summary		Student pages 59–63
INTRODUCTION	Review homework.	Review homework from Day 19.
CLASSWORK	Check Your Work For Further Reflection	Student self-assessment: Find the volume of prisms and cylinders.

Additional Resources: Additional Practice, Section E, Student Book pages 68 and 69

Materials

Student Resources

No resources required

Teachers Resources

No resources required

Student Materials

Quantities listed are per student, unless otherwise noted.

- Calculators
- Centimeter graph paper (three sheets)
- Empty tissue boxes (one per group of students)
- Scissors

* See Hints and Comments for optional materials.

Learning Lines

Surface Area and Volume

To develop students' understanding of the concept of volume, they fill packages with cubes. The surface area is how much covering is needed to wrap all the sides of a package. Nets of packages are used to find the surface area.

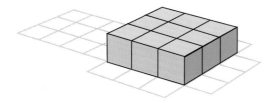

In this section, students explore relationships between surface area and volume. They discover that shapes with the same volume can have different surface areas. To support the development of students' understanding of the concept of volume, finding the volume of a solid in cubic centimeters is related to the question, *How many centimeter cubes fit in the shape?*

To find the volume of a shape, students will progress from:

- informal, counting the number of centimeter cubes in one layer and then counting the number of layers, to
- pre-formal, the number of centimeter cubes in the length times the number of centimeter cubes in the width times the number of layers, to
- formal, *volume = length × width × height*.

Volume is expressed using both metric and customary units.

Strategies

In previous sections, students developed strategies for finding area, for example:

- dividing shapes into smaller parts whose area is more easily found;
- enclosing shapes in rectangles and subtracting the area of the "extra" parts; and
- using formulas.

Similar strategies can be used for finding volume:

- dividing solids into smaller parts whose volume is more easily found;
- enclosing solids in rectangular blocks and subtracting the volume of the "extra" parts; and
- using formulas.

At the End of This Section: Learning Outcomes

Students are able to find the volume of shapes using informal as well as formal strategies. For example, they can find volumes by counting "unit" blocks or by reshaping irregular shapes.

Students have developed an understanding of when and how to use the formula *Volume = area of slice × height*. They understand the relationship between volume and surface area.

E Surface Area and Volume

Notes

Discuss what *surface area* means. Discuss the relationship between surface area and volume. Use a cardboard box or a chocolate bar with its wrapper as examples.

1a The clay is the volume (fills the space inside); the wrapping paper is the surface area.

1b Encourage students to explain their answer precisely.

Surface Area and Volume

Packages

In Section D you investigated the relationship between perimeter and area.

In a similar way, you can look at the relationship between **surface area** and **volume**. This is like comparing the amount of wrapping paper you need to cover a package with the space inside the package.

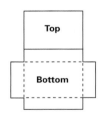

Here are two different packages of modeling clay, drawn to the same scale.

1. **a.** Which package do you think has more clay? Why?

    b. Which package do you think needs more wrapping paper? Why?

The area covered with wrapping paper is the surface area of the package. The top, bottom, and sides are the surfaces or faces.

A packaging machine cuts and folds cardboard packages.

Here is one gift package and the cardboard to make the package. The drawing of the cardboard that can be folded to make the package is called a **net**.

The packages can be filled with cubes.

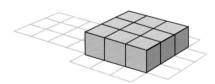

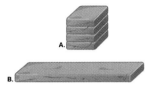

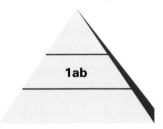
Reaching All Learners

Vocabulary Building

Have students add *surface area* and *net* to the vocabulary section of their notebook with illustrations. Some students might want to attach an example of a net to the notebook.

Intervention

Provide models of three-dimensional solids and nets (candy bar, gift box, cereal box, pudding box, and so on). Have students make a net to fit 9 centimeter cubes using graph paper.

Solutions and Samples

1. a. The amount of modeling clay is the same.

Sample explanation:

If you cut the long bar into four equal pieces and stack them, you can see that this is true.

b. The long bar needs more wrapping paper.

Sample explanation:

The cube-shaped package has six sides that have about the same area. Use one of these sides to cover the long bar. You need four of them to cover the top of the long bar and four to cover the bottom. So you need at least 8 of these parts for the bottom and top.

Hints and Comments

Materials

centimeter cubes, optional (nine per group of students);
centimeter graph paper, optional (one sheet per student);
scissors, optional (one pair per student)

Overview

Students compare two packages of modeling clay with respect to the amount of clay and with respect to the amount of wrapping paper. Students are introduced to the concept of *surface area* of a package and to the concept of a *net*.

About the Mathematics

In this unit, students may describe shapes using informal language. For example, what students may now refer to as a "side" is formally defined as a "face." In the unit *Packages and Polygons*, mathematical language will be introduced. In that unit, students will make and investigate nets for different three-dimensional shapes.

Planning

You may start with a review of what students discovered in Section D:

- two shapes with the same perimeter can have different areas; and
- two shapes with the same area can have different perimeters.

Then you may have students read and work on problem 1 in small groups. Discuss their answers and explanations. Then you may have students read the information below problem 1. They may continue to problem 2 on the next page, or have them do the extension first.

Extension

This extension previews the problems on the next page and is especially meant as an extra activity for those students who have problems in reading and interpreting two-dimensional drawings of three-dimensional situations.

Students can work in pairs or small groups; each group makes an arrangement of nine cubes like the drawing on the page. On centimeter graph paper, each student draws a net that can be cut out and folded into a package for this arrangement of nine cubes. Students can use the cubes to check their nets.

E Surface Area and Volume

Notes

2 Allow students to use centimeter cubes if they need to.

2b Draw a net that corresponds to the cube size you are using. Use centimeter graph paper if you use centimeter cubes.

Students can model how they figured out the number of cubes for packages A to D.

Packages are classified by the maximum number of cubes that each can hold.

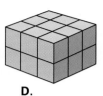

A. B. C. D.

2. **a.** How many cubes will fit into each package?

   b. On graph paper, draw a net for each package.

   c. Which package requires the least cardboard material to make? Show your work.

The packaging machine makes many different-sized packages.

3. Is it possible to make a package to hold exactly 100 cubes?

   If your answer is "yes," give the dimensions of this package.

   If your answer is "no," explain why the machine is unable to make this package.

Here is the bottom area for a new package. The package will have a height of 4 cubes.

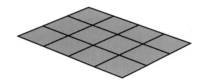

4. How many cubes will fit into this package?

Assessment Pyramid

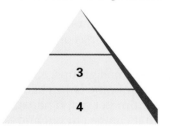

Reason about the dimensions for a package with a given volume.

Visualize geometric models to find volume.

Reaching All Learners

Intervention

Model clay samples with clay, centimeter cubes, sugar cubes, or one inch blocks.

Extension

For problem 3, have students give as many different possible packages as they can.

Solutions and Samples

2. a. 9 cubes fit in A.

8 cubes fit in B.

12 cubes fit in C.

18 cubes fit in D.

b. Sample drawings:

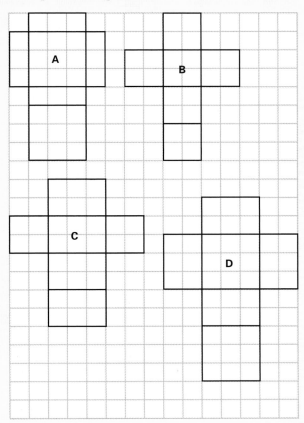

c. B needs the least cardboard.

A. $9 + 9 + 4 \times 3 = 18 + 12 = 30$

B. $6 \times 4 = 24$

C. $4 \times 6 + 2 \times 4 = 24 + 8 = 32$

D. $2 \times 9 + 4 \times 6 = 18 + 24 = 42$

3. Yes, it is possible. The package should be 10 by 10 by 1.

4. On the bottom layer there are $3 \times 4 = 12$ cubes, and there are four layers. So the total is $4 \times 12 = 48$ cubes.

Hints and Comments

Materials

centimeter graph paper (one or two sheets per student); centimeter cubes, optional (20 per group of students); scissors, optional (one pair per student)

Overview

Students make nets for different packages and determine which packages require the least cardboard material. Then they solve problems about packages and numbers of cubes.

About the Mathematics

These problems are meant to further develop students' spatial visualization skills and understanding of the concept of volume.

Planning

You may have students work on problems 2–4 individually or in small groups.

Comments About the Solutions

2. b. Students can check their nets by comparing them to those of other students and/or cutting out and folding the nets and comparing their shapes to the drawings in the Student Book. (Hint: Comparing will be easier if students fold the net with the gridlines on the outside.)

c. Without making all the calculations, students may reason that D needs more cardboard than A (D is twice as high) and C needs more cardboard than B (because C is larger than B). So you only have to find the areas for A and B and compare them.

E Surface Area and Volume

Notes

5b Provide groups with tissue boxes that are similar or other boxes that are a similar size.

6 Discuss how 1 cm³ relates to 1 cm × 1 cm × 1 cm and have students draw the 1-cm cube in their notebook.

7 Encourage students to use the centimeter cubes. Making a table to list the solutions can help students find all the possible different-sized boxes.

7a If students do not create a table of length, width, and height, perhaps this could be shown.

Measuring Inside

You can make a centimeter cube by drawing a figure like this and folding it into a cube. Each edge of the cube must measure exactly 1 cm.

The figure is called the *net* of a cube.

5. **a.** Use centimeter graph paper to draw a net of a centimeter cube.

   Cut it out and fold it to make one cubic centimeter. You don't need to paste it together.

   b. Cut the top off a tissue box. How many cubic centimeters are needed to fill it? Explain how you found your answer.

A cube with dimensions 1 cm by 1 cm by 1 cm is said to have a **volume** of 1 cubic centimeter, written as 1 cm³.

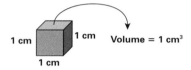

6. What is the surface area of the centimeter cube?

A rectangular package that will hold exactly 24 cubes of 1 cm by 1 cm by 1 cm has a volume of 24 cm³.

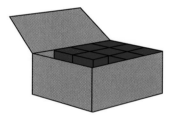

7. **a.** Use centimeter cubes to find as many different-sized packages as you can that will hold exactly 24 cubes. Use dimensions that are counting numbers.

Reaching All Learners

Vocabulary Building

Volume is a new vocabulary word that should be added to this section of the student notebook. As a class, have students decide on a definition and draw an illustration to represent their understanding of volume. Students can share their illustrations with others.

Intervention

Use solid centimeter cubes to model this problem, but do not provide enough cubes to fill the box.

Extension

The net at the top of the page is not the only possible one for a centimeter cube. Have students draw others.

Solutions and Samples

5. a. See student drawings of nets.

   b. Students should measure the length, width, and height of the box and use these measurements to determine how many centimeter cubes will fit on the bottom and how many layers there are. Sample response:

      My tissue box measures 5 cm × 11 cm × 23 cm. The bottom layer requires 253 cubes and with five layers; there would be 253 × 5 or 1,265 cubes.

6. 6 cm^2. Sample response:

     There are six sides, each with an area of 1 square centimeter, so the area is 6 × 1 = 6 square centimeters.

7. a.

Length	Width	Height
12	2	1
6	4	1
4	3	2
6	2	2
24	1	1
8	3	1

Hints and Comments

Materials

centimeter graph paper (one sheet per student); scissors (one pair per student); empty tissue boxes (one per group of students); centimeter cubes, optional (24 per pair or groups of students)

Overview

Students make a one-centimeter cube. They learn its volume is one cubic centimeter. They find out how many cubic centimeters fit in a tissue box. Then students find different-sized packages, all with a volume of 24 cm^3.

About the Mathematics

The numbers that students find as dimensions are each a factor of 24. In the unit *Facts and Factors*, students will learn strategies to find all factors of a number.

Planning

Have students work in pairs or small groups on problems 5 and 6. Briefly discuss students' results in class. Then students can work in small groups on problem 7, which is continued on the next page.

Comments About the Solutions

   5. b. Students should realize that they do not need to fill the box with cubic centimeters. They can use the cubic centimeters they made to find out how many fit along the length and the width of the box (multiplying these numbers will give the number of cubic centimeters in one layer), and then they can use centimeter cubes to find out how many layers will fit into the box.

   7. a. Here students may discover that they can find the number of cubes that fit inside the package by multiplying the length × width × height. This would lead to a discussion of how finding volume relates to finding area (see also problem 4 on Student Book page 50). If they do not make this discovery on their own, hold off discussing this until they have finished problem 8 on the next page.

E Surface Area and Volume

Notes

Note that the volume label is a cubic unit, and the surface area label is a square unit.

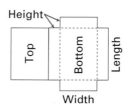

b. Determine how much cardboard is needed to make each package. Do not include cardboard for flaps to paste the edges together. Use a table like the one below to record your results.

Package Dimensions				
Length (in cm)	Width (in cm)	Height (in cm)	Volume (in cm³)	Surface Area (in cm²)
			24	
			24	
			24	
			24	
			24	
			24	

Maria is trying to find the volume of this package. The package has been partially filled with cubes. Maria says, "I can easily find the volume of this package! The bottom of the package measures 8 cm by 7 cm. I can fit 56 cubes on the bottom layer…"

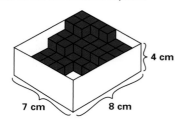

4 cm

7 cm   8 cm

8. a. Explain what else Maria has to do to find the volume of the package.

b. What is the volume of Maria's package?

8a Packages of the same volume do not necessarily have the same surface areas, although a package with dimensions 4 × 3 × 2 is the same as a package with dimensions 2 × 3 × 4. Discuss how this can occur. In this chart, find packages with totally different cube dimensions.

8b Discuss how to find surface area. Model the first package with students or have them share how to find this measurement in groups or as a class. This concept was previously taught as "area" and is now being applied to finding the area of surfaces.

Assessment Pyramid

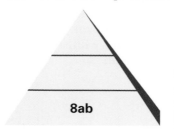

8ab

Find volumes by counting unit blocks.

Reaching All Learners

Intervention

Use the centimeter net to show this model vs. a pudding box that overlaps. You may have students draw a net on graph paper for each package they find. Model that 4 × 3 × 2 is the same as 2 × 3 × 4 and 3 × 4 × 2, and so on. Use cubes to do Maria's problem. Expand the chart so that it includes 6 columns for surface area faces and a total surface area column.

Advanced Learners

Ask, *If you were going to cover the packages to sell, which package uses the least cover material?* Have students relate their findings to chocolate bar wrappers. Ask, *Generally, which is the least expensive to wrap?* Have samples or ask students to obtain samples of different-sized candy bars to explain this information.

Solutions and Samples

7. b. Tables will vary. Sample student response:

Package Dimensions				
Length (in cm)	Width (in cm)	Height (in cm)	Volume (in cm³)	Surface Area (in cm²)
12	2	1	24	76
6	4	1	24	68
4	3	2	24	52
6	2	2	24	56
24	1	1	24	98
8	3	1	24	70

8 a. Maria has to multiply the 56 cubes in the bottom layer by four to find the total number of cubes.

b. The volume of the package is $56 \times 4 = 224$ cubic centimeters, or 224 cm³.

Hints and Comments

Materials

centimeter cubes, optional (24 per pair or groups of students)

Overview

Students find the surface area of each package. Then they explain how to find the volume of a package that is partially filled with cubes.

About the Mathematics

Area can be used to describe the surface area of a three-dimensional solid as well as a two-dimensional shape. Problem 7 (which begins on page 51) illustrates that volume and surface area are not directly proportional. For example, each of the two shapes shown here has a volume of 8 cubic units. Solid A has a surface area of 34 square units, while the surface area of B is 24 square units.

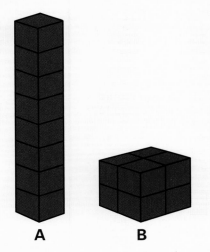

A   B

Planning

Students finish problem 7 working in small groups. Check students' responses in class. You may ask students to think about the box with the smallest surface area and the one with the largest surface area. (The more a box resembles a cube, the smaller its surface area.) Then you may have students work individually on problem 8, and use this problem as informal assessment.

Comments About the Solutions

7. b. Encourage students to calculate the surface area of each package in a systematic way. For example:

Area top and bottom = 2 × …

Area left and right side = 2 × …

Area front and back side = 2 × …

E Surface Area and Volume

Notes

11b, 12a and b
Compile the class statements and work together to discern which are accurate and post these in the classroom. Students can add to this list as they work through Section E. Parents would be excellent resources for adding to this list.

Jonathan bought a special vase for his friend Erin who lives in Ireland. He needs to pack the vase very carefully so that he can mail it overseas. His shipping box measures 35 cm by 16 cm and has a height of 10 cm. He bought a sack of packaging material to protect and cushion the vase. The guarantee on the sack claims it "will fill a box as a big as 6,000 cubic centimeters."

9. Will this be enough packaging material to keep the vase safe? Show your work.

To measure the volume of larger packages, you use larger sized cubes. In the metric system, you use cubic decimeters or cubic meters. This drawing represents one cubic decimeter (dm^3). Note that one decimeter (dm) = 10 cm.

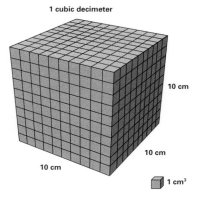

1 cubic decimeter

10 cm
10 cm
10 cm

1 cm³

10. a. If everyone in your class made a cubic centimeter, would it be enough to fill 1 dm^3?

b. How many cubic centimeters are needed to fill 1 dm^3?

11. a. Name some objects whose volume would be measured in cubic decimeters; cubic meters.

b. Write four statements about how cubic centimeters, cubic decimeters, and cubic meters are related.

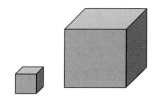

The cubes to the left represent a cubic inch and a cubic foot, two customary units of measure for volume.

12. a. Write a statement about how cubic inches and cubic feet are related.

b. Write two other statements about how cubic feet and cubic yards are related.

Assessment Pyramid

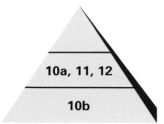

10a, 11, 12

10b

Find volumes by counting unit blocks and use metric and customary system.

Reaching All Learners

Intervention

Use centimeter cubes and models to represent 1 dm, 1 dm^3, 1 cm, 1 cm^3, 1 in. and 1 in^3. Also, create actual models of 1 m^3, 1 ft^3, and 1 yd^3. (Refrigerator boxes or other large boxes may be available for these models.) Students need to see these sizes to make connections.

Parental Involvement

Ask, *What might be measured in in^3, ft^3, or yd^3?* Parents would be excellent resources to help with this investigation.

Solutions and Samples

9. Yes, more than enough. Sample explanation:

To find the volume of the box, I filled it with centimeter cubes. On the bottom, I was able to fit 35 × 16, or 560 centimeter cubes. Since the box can hold 10 layers, the total number of centimeter cubes that fit in the box is 10 × 560 = 5,600.

The volume of the box is 5,600 cm^3. The packing material will fill 6,000 cm^3. So the packing material will definitely fill the box (especially since the vase will be packed in there as well).

10. a. No, because to cover the bottom of one cubic decimeter, you already need 10 × 10 = 100 cubic centimeters. Cubes made by one class would not even fill a single layer.

b. It would take 1,000 cubic centimeters to fill a cubic decimeter (which is 10 cm × 10 cm × 10 cm).

11. a. Sample responses:

Cubic decimeters: a refrigerator, the trunk of a car

Cubic meters: a large container, a truck, a house, grain, or water

b. One cubic decimeter is 1,000 cubic centimeters (10 layers of 10 × 10 cubic centimeters).

One cubic meter is 1,000 cubic decimeters (10 layers of 10 × 10 cubic decimeters).

One cubic meter is 1,000,000 cubic centimeters (100 layers of 100 × 100 cubic centimeters).

12. a. One cubic foot is 1,728 cubic inches (12 layers of 144 cubic inches).

b. One cubic yard is 27 cubic feet (three layers of nine cubic feet).

Hints and Comments

Materials

calculators (one per student)

Overview

Students investigate whether a sack of packing material is enough to fill a package with given dimensions. Then they find relationships within the metric and customary units for volume.

About the Mathematics

In the metric system, volume is measured in cubic centimeters, cubic decimeters, and cubic meters. A cubic decimeter is the same as one liter, which is used for liquids. Students will investigate this relationship in the unit *Packages and Polygons*.

Planning

You may have students work on problems 9 and 10 in small groups. Discuss their responses. You may have students work individually on problems 11 and 12. Allow students to use a calculator to make their computations.

Comments About the Solutions

10.–12.

Students need the relationships within the metric and customary units for length from Section C. If you see students struggling, you may want to review these relationships.

Observe whether students start to shorten their calculations; for example, do they count all the unit blocks that cover the bottom and then count the number of layers, or do they already calculate: the number of unit blocks in the length × number of unit blocks in the width × number of unit blocks in the height? Or maybe just *length × width × height?* You may discuss the different strategies that are used in class so that students may learn from each others' strategies.

E Surface Area and Volume

Notes

Reshaping

These solids are made of cubic centimeter blocks.

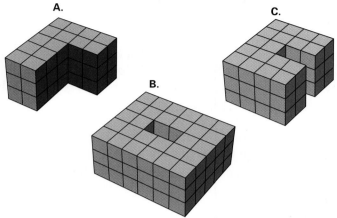

A.

C.

B.

13. Find the volume of each solid and describe your solution strategy.

13 Have the class create a list of strategies for finding volume as a review:

- use the formula;
- divide the shape into smaller cubes and find those volumes and then recombine;
- find one layer and multiply that times the number of layers; and
- some other strategy.

Students can put these strategies in their notebook.

14b Students can share which strategy was used.

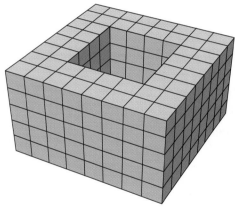

14. a. Describe two different strategies to find the volume of the shape above.

b. Use one of these strategies to find the volume.

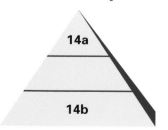

Assessment Pyramid

14a

14b

Generalize procedures for determining volume.

Use blocks and visualize geometric models to find volume.

Reaching All Learners

Intervention

Create smaller models or a simpler problem; for example, remove the outside level, or begin with 1 cm in height or model the shape with cubes. Then divide into smaller solids, figure those volumes, and combine to find the total volume.

Accommodation

Make a chart to systematically find the length, width, height, and total in columns. Make a cubic centimeter model that students can see and touch.

Solutions and Samples

13. The volume of **A** is 42 cubic centimeters.

The volume of **B** is 84 cubic centimeters.

The volume of **C** is 54 cubic centimeters.

Sample strategies:

- Cut a solid in parts and calculate the number of cubes in each of the parts. Then add, or paste, the parts into one large block. (This strategy resembles what students did with reallotting area.)
- Count the number of cubes in one layer, and then multiply by number of layers.

14. a. Some possible strategies are:

- Count the number of cubes in one layer and then multiply that by the number of layers.
- Calculate the total number of cubes when the hole in the middle is filled. Then calculate the number of cubes in the hole in the middle and subtract that from the total number of cubes.
- Cut the shape into smaller block-shaped parts. Then find the volume of each block and add them together.

b. Sample calculations:

- There are 48 cubes in one layer, and there are 5 layers, so the total number of blocks is $48 \times 5 = 240$. The volume is 240 cubic centimeters.
- The number of cubes in the solid when it is filled is $8 \times 8 \times 5 = 320$ cubic centimeters.

  The number of cubes in the hole in the middle is $4 \times 4 \times 5 = 80$ cubic centimeters.

  $320-80 = 240$ cubes, so the volume is 240 cubic centimeters.

- Cut the shape into four smaller parts. For example, cut the large shape into two blocks of 8 by 2 by 5 cubes and two blocks of 4 by 2 by 5 cubes. This would make two blocks of 80 cubes and two blocks of 40 cubes. Overall, this would be $2 \times 80 + 2 \times 40 = 160 + 80 = 240$ cubes, so the total volume is 240 cubic centimeters. (Note that there are different possibilities for cutting this shape into smaller parts.)

Hints and Comments

Overview

Students develop and describe strategies for finding the volume of irregular solids built of centimeter cubes.

About the Mathematics

In previous sections, students developed strategies for finding area, for example:

- dividing shapes in smaller parts whose area is more easily found, and
- enclosing shapes in rectangles and subtracting the areas of the "extra" parts.

Similar strategies can be used for finding volume:

- dividing solids in smaller parts whose volume is more easily found, and
- enclosing solids in rectangular blocks and subtracting the volumes of the "extra" parts.

Planning

You may have students work on problems 13 and 14 individually or in small groups. You may use problem 14 as informal assessment and/or assign as homework. Be sure to discuss students' answers and strategies to problem 13, preferably before students start working on problem 14.

Comments About the Solutions

13. You may encourage students to use relationships between the shapes. They may find for example:

- Shape **B** can be made by doubling shape **A**.
- Shape **C** can be made by adding a block of 2 by 2 by 3 cubes to shape **A**.
- Shape **C** can be made by subtracting a block of 5 by 2 by 3 from shape **B**.

14. A sophisticated way to find the number of cubes in one layer might be:

Calculate 8×8, as if the layer were filled; then subtract 4×4 for the hole in the middle.

E Surface Area and Volume

Notes

Note that volume labels are cubic units.

Make sure students recognize that the soda can is a *cylinder*.

15 Students can work in groups and identify the strategy used. Then groups can demonstrate their methods.

15 Students should recognize that the volume of shape G is difficult to figure because it starts wide and then comes to a point. The shape's name is a *square pyramid*. Its volume is more complicated to figure. A square pyramid with height *h* and base side length *l* has volume of $\frac{l^2h}{3}$. Three of these square pyramids make a cube; students can estimate this volume.

A.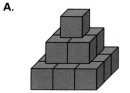

B.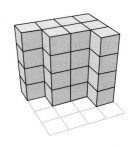

C.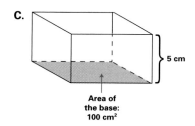

Area of the base: 100 cm²

5 cm

D. Your classroom

E. The stack of boards below.

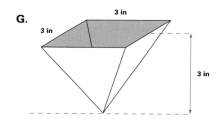

1 m
20 cm
30 cm

F. A soda can.

G.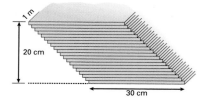

3 in
3 in
3 in

15. Find the volume of each item and describe your strategy.

Solutions and Samples

15. A. The volume is $9 + 4 + 1 = 14$ cubes.

Sample explanation of the strategy:

Just count the cubes in each layer.

B. The volume is 32 cubes.

Sample strategy:

$4 \times 4 \times 4 = 64$ is the volume of double the solid shown. So the volume of the solid is $64 \div 2 = 32$.

C. The volume is 500 cm^3.

Strategy will vary. Sample strategy:

The area of the base is 100 cm^2. This means that there are 100 cubes that make up the bottom layer. The box will hold 5 layers of 100 cubes, so its volume is 500 cubic centimeters.

D. Answers may vary, depending on whether the dimensions were estimated or measured. Sample strategy:

First I measured the length and the width of the floor so I could calculate how many cubic feet would fit on the floor. Then I estimated how many layers would fit in the height of the classroom.

E. The volume is 60,000 cm^3.

Sample strategies:

- Students may calculate the volume of 1 plank ($30 \times 100 \times 1$) and do this 20 times.

- Another strategy is finding the area of the front side, the parallelogram base $\times$ height $= 20 \times 30 = 600$ cm^2 and multiply this by 100 cm.

- A third strategy is to straighten the stack, which does not affect the volume, then compute the volume of the rectangular block by multiplying $100 \times 30 \times 20$.

F. Answers will vary depending on the size of the can. Sample response:

By counting squares on graph paper, I found that the area of the circle is about 35 cm^2. Since the can is 12 cm high, the total volume is about 420 cm^3.

G. Answers will vary. Sample response:

The volume is less than $3 \times 3 \times 3 = 27$ cubic inches it is. I estimate about half of that, so it is about 13 cubic inches.

Hints and Comments

Overview

Students find the volume of different shapes and describe their strategies.

About the Mathematics

It is important that students develop an understanding of the concept of volume. To find the volume of a rectangular block in cubic centimeters, students may think of: *How many centimeter cubes fit in the shape?*

Allow students to progress at their own pace from:

- informal, counting the number of centimeter cubes in one layer and then counting the number of layers, to

- pre-formal, the number of centimeter cubes in the length times the number of centimeter cubes in the width times the number of layers, and finally to

- formal: *volume = length × width × height.*

Planning

Students may work on problem 15 in small groups. Discuss their responses and strategies.

Comments About the Solutions

15. D. Students may use meters or feet in estimating or measuring, so the volume will be in cubic meters or cubic feet.

G. An estimate is all that is expected at this point. The volume of this pyramid is actually one third of the cube with sides of 3 by 3 by 3 inches. Students will investigate how to find the volume of a pyramid in the unit *Packages and Polygons.*

E Surface Area and Volume

Notes

If an object has a shape that can be cut in **slices** that all have the same size, you can calculate the volume of the object in an easy way, by using the formula:

volume = area of a slice × height

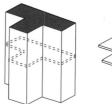

16b Students can draw one slice for each shape and identify its area in their notebooks. Check whether they draw the slice correctly: not a three dimensional drawing but a top view.

16. **a.** For which items from problem 15 can you use this volume formula?

   b. For each of the items you chose, describe the shape of the slice. What is the area of each slice for each item you chose?

17. Explain why the formula doesn't work for a cone and a pyramid.

18a Review how to find the area of a circle. Students draw the can slice in their notebook and show its area.

The can has a height of 16 cm, and the diameter of a slice is 6 cm.

18. **a.** Calculate the area of a slice.

   b. Use your answer from **a** to calculate the volume of the can.

   c. Find a can in the shape of a cylinder with different dimensions that has the same volume.

18c If students struggle with this problem, you may suggest changing the diameter and then adjusting the height. Due to rounding of the volume in problem b, students may not get a precise answer. When discussing this problem, you may ask students why it doesn't work when you halve the diameter and double the height.

Reaching All Learners

Vocabulary Building

A *Slice* as the area of a shape and also the formula for volume using the slice method should be added to the student notebooks.

Extension

Have students find the volume of a triangular prism using the slice method. They review how to find the area of a triangle and draw this illustration or find an example.

Have students think of two other solids in which the slice method will not work to find the volume. (Answer: *sphere, hemisphere, triangular pyramid*)

0Solutions and Samples

16. a. The volume formula can be used for **C**, **D** (probably), **E**, and **F**.

b. The shape of the slice for each of these items is as follows:

C. rectangle

D. rectangle

E. rectangle

F. circle

The area for each slice is:

C. 100 cm²

D. This depends on the dimensions of the classroom. Most likely the area of the slice would be whatever the area of the classroom floor or ceiling is.

E. 3,000 cm²

F. The area of the base of the soda can is π × radius × radius.

17. The slices for the cone and pyramid do not have the same size as you move from the bottom to the top of the shape.

18. a. *area of slice* = π × radius × radius.

In this case, the radius is 3, so the area is π × 3 × 3 ≈28.3 cm².

b. *volume* = *area of slice* × *height* = 28.3 × 16 ≈ 453 cm³.

c. Answers may vary. Sample answer:

I doubled the diameter, so the radius became 6. Then I calculated the area of the slice: π × 6 × 6 ≈ 113.

I looked at what the height must be to get 453. Since 4 × 113 = 452, the height is about 4 cm.

Hints and Comments

Overview

Students learn and apply a formula for finding the volume of a shape that can be cut in slices that all have the same size.

About the Mathematics

The formula, *Volume = length × width × height*, can only be used for rectangular blocks. The formula, *Volume = area of a slice × height*, can be used for a wider range of shapes. Students informally used this idea when they calculated the volume of the stack of boards in previous problems.

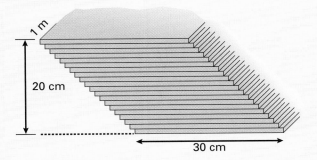

Planning

Discuss the text on top of Student Book page 56 in class. Then you may have students work on problems 16–18 in small groups.

Comments About the Solutions

18. c. You may show how different possibilities can be found using the formula without using a calculator.

Volume = area of a slice × height, so for the can:

Volume = π × radius × radius × height, or

Volume = π × 3 × 3 × 16.

This is the same as *Volume = π × 9 × 4 × 4*, or

Volume = π × 4 × 4 × 9.

This is the volume of a can with a radius of 4 and a height of 9.

You may now challenge students to use this idea to find more possibilities.

Sample possibilities:

Volume = π × 2 × 2 × 36

Volume = π × 1 × 1 × 144

Volume = π × 12 × 12 × 1

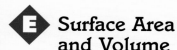

Surface Area and Volume

Notes

Review the use of the area model to find the surface area of this slice when the dimensions are mixed numbers.

Be sure the volume labels are cubic units.

19 Students may want to use graph paper so they can draw a slice of the shape for finding its area.

All slices of this container are rectangles with the same dimensions.

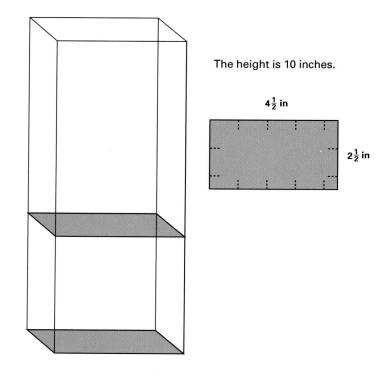

The height is 10 inches.

$4\frac{1}{2}$ in

$2\frac{1}{2}$ in

19. a. Name a use for this container.

  b. Calculate the volume of the container. Show your work.

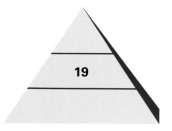

Assessment Pyramid

19

Compute volume and recognize when and how to use the formula
$V = $ *area of slice* $\times$ *height.*

Reaching All Learners

Intervention

Have students draw the container slice in their notebook or on graph paper and figure the surface area of this slice. (They can refer back to the area model in Section C or convert the mixed numbers into decimals.)

Extension

Have students find the volume of some other containers that have this shape (refrigerator box, aquarium, storage cabinet).

Solutions and Samples

19. a. Answers will vary. This container could be used to pack cereal or some other type of food.

b. The volume is $112\frac{1}{2}$ cubic inches.

Sample calculations:

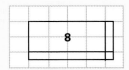

The area of the slice is $4\frac{1}{2} \times 2\frac{1}{2} = 8 + 3 + \frac{1}{4} = 11\frac{1}{4}$ square inches.

The volume of the container is *area of slice × height* $= 11\frac{1}{4} \times 10 = 112\frac{1}{2}$ cubic inches.

Hints and Comments

Materials

graph paper, optional (one sheet per student)

Overview

Students calculate the volume of a container that has mixed fractions as side lengths of a slice.

Planning

Students may work individually on this problem, so you may use it as informal assessment.

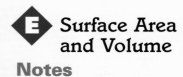
This container is $4\frac{1}{2}$ in. high.
The base of this container is 10 in. by $2\frac{1}{2}$ in.

You can replace the words "area of slice" with the words "area of base."

20. **a.** Rewrite the volume formula using the word *base*.

   b. Calculate the volume of this container.

   c. Compare your answer to your answer for problem 19. What do you notice? Explain.

A container has dimensions of $1\frac{1}{2}$ in. by $2\frac{1}{2}$ in. by 6 in.

21. Calculate the volume of this container.

A gift box has a volume of 240 cm³.

22. **a.** What dimensions does this gift box have? Find three different possibilities. Note: The box does not need to have the shape of a block.

   b. Name two objects that have about this same volume.

   c. **Reflect** Does every gift box that has a volume of 240 cm³ have the same surface area? Explain your thinking. Use your examples from part **a** to support your answer with calculations.

22a Consider setting up this problem with a chart to show length, width, and height dimensions, like the one on page 52.

22c Revisit the chart on page 52, which shows volume and surface area measurements. Note that all surface areas were different even though the volume was the same.

Assessment Pyramid

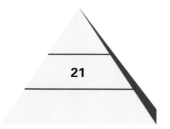

21

Compute volume and recognize when and how to use the formula
$V = $ *area of slice* × *height*.

Reaching All Learners

Intervention

For problem 21, have students draw this container in their notebook and label the dimensions. This container's slice area could be found by using the area model method and then if multiplied by the height, would result in the volume.

Accommodation

Type the steps to find the volume by the slice method or by using the formula. Post another area model example for students to see how to find a slice with mixed numbers.

Extension

After completing problem 21, ask, *Name two different items that could fit in a box this size.*

Solutions and Samples

20. a. *volume = area of base × height.*

b. area base $= 10 \times 2\frac{1}{2} = 25$ in^2.
volume = area of base × height
$= 25 \times 4\frac{1}{2} = 100 + 12\frac{1}{2} = 112\frac{1}{2}$ in^3.

c. The answers are the same; actually the containers have the same dimensions, just different bases! The volume of the second one was easier to calculate.

21. The volume is $22\frac{1}{2}$ in^3.

Different strategies are possible:

- Using the side with dimensions $1\frac{1}{2}$ in. by 6 in. as base:

  The area of the base is $1\frac{1}{2} \times 6 = 9$ in^2.

  The volume of the container is $9 \times 2\frac{1}{2} = 18 + 4\frac{1}{2} = 22\frac{1}{2}$ in^3.

- Using the side with dimensions $2\frac{1}{2}$ in. by 6 in. as base:

  The area of the base is $2\frac{1}{2} \times 6 = 15$ in^2.

  The volume $= 15 \times 1\frac{1}{2} = 15 + 7\frac{1}{2} = 22\frac{1}{2}$ in^3.

22. a. The box could have several dimensions.

Sample solutions:

10 cm by 6 cm by 4 cm.

5 cm by 6 cm by 8 cm.

5 cm by 12 cm by 4 cm.

b. A mini water bottle (one fourth of a liter) and a half-pint milk carton are about the same volume as this box.

c. No. Sample explanation:

The box with dimensions 10 cm by 6 cm by 4 cm has a surface area of $2 \times 60 + 2 \times 24 + 2 \times 40 = 248$ cm^2.

The box with dimensions 5 cm by 6 cm by 8 cm has a surface area of $2 \times 30 + 2 \times 48 + 2 \times 40 = 236$ cm^2.

The box with dimensions 5 cm by 12 cm by 4 cm has a surface area of $2 \times 60 + 2 \times 48 + 2 \times 20 = 256$ cm^2.

Hints and Comments

Overview

Students rewrite and use the formula using area of base instead of area of slice. They find possible dimensions of a box with a given volume.

Planning

Students may work on problems 20–22 individually or in small groups. Problem 21 may be used as informal assessment. You may want to discuss problem 20 in class before students continue with problem 21.

Comments About the Solutions

20. This problem shows that you can choose a different base and still find the same volume. This is easy to understand: just turn the shape so it gets a different side as base.

21. From the previous problem, students should understand that they could use a base of which the area can easily be calculated.

E Surface Area and Volume

Notes

If there is time, it might be of interest to students to model Archimedes' strategy for finding *pi*.

Math History

History of π

π is one of the most ancient numbers known in history. It represents the most famous ratio in mathematics, the ratio of the circumference of a circle to its diameter.

You can use a calculator to find the value for π. But what did people use in earlier days?

Long ago, people used the number 3. That is not very accurate, but it was easy to use for their calculations.

The Babylonians used a more accurate value: $3 + \frac{1}{8}$.

In the Egyptian Rhind Papyrus, which is dated about 1650 B.C., the value for π was calculated as $4 \times \frac{8}{9} \times \frac{8}{9}$.

About 250 B.C., the famous ancient Greek mathematician and inventor Archimedes used the following strategy.

He constructed **polygons** with six sides in and around the circle, like you see here. He knew how to calculate the circumference of both polygons. Then he doubled the number of sides (12), and doubled again and again until he had polygons with 96 sides! He then computed the perimeter of these polygons and found the value of π to lie between $\frac{223}{71}$ and $\frac{22}{7}$.

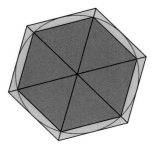

In the fifth century, the Chinese mathematician Zu Chungzhi found a different value for Archimedes' $\frac{223}{71}$. That more accurate value was $\frac{355}{113}$, and six decimals of π were now known.

This record lasted until 1400, when the Persian mathematician Al-Kashi calculated a value with 16 decimals. He used Archimedes' strategy, but he doubled the number of sides 23 times.

William Jones, an English mathematician, introduced the modern symbol for pi in 1700. The letter π was chosen because π in Greek, pronounced like our letter "p," stands for "perimeter."

As a result of the development of technology, the known decimals for pi have now exceeded 1 trillion.

So the number of times a diameter fits around its circle is

3.14159265358979323846264338327950288419716939937551….

Reaching All Learners

Extension

Have students recreate Archimedes' attempts to estimate π using the figure show on this page as a model. Have students make their own (large) circle with a protractor or compass card, marking every 30 degrees along the edge of the circle. By connecting every other 30 degree mark, students can create a hexagon that inscribes the circle. The remaining marks can be used to create the hexagon that circumscribes the circle. Using a centimeter ruler, have students measure the lengths of the sides for each hexagon to the nearest millimeter. Add up the side measures for each hexagon to find a rough approximation for π.

Hints and Comments

Extension

You may assign students to place all the different values that have been used for the number that we now know as π on a number line. Have calculators available for this assignment. You may write these different values on index cards and hang them on a number line in the classroom.

Surface Area and Volume

Notes

After reading the Summary aloud with students, have them come up with two questions whose answers can be found on this page. Take time for the asking and answering of these questions in small groups or the whole class. This will help you assess basic student understanding of volume and surface area.

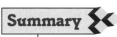 Surface Area and Volume

Summary

In this section, you studied packages. Packages have a surface area and a volume.

The surface area is how much covering you need to wrap all the faces of a package. Surface area is measured using square measuring units.

The surface area of this package is 32 square units.

The volume of a package indicates how many cubes totally fill up a package.

To measure the volume of a package, you can count or calculate how many cubic units fit inside the package.

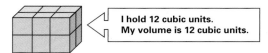

I hold 12 cubic units.
My volume is 12 cubic units.

Volume is measured using cubic measuring units. One common measuring unit for volume is a cubic centimeter (cm^3).

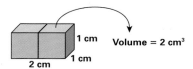

1 cm
2 cm
1 cm
Volume = 2 cm^3

You investigated relationships between surface area and volume. You learned that two objects with the same volume can have different surface areas.

   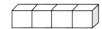

Volume is 4 cm^3.
Surface area is 16 cm^2.

Volume is 4 cm^3.
Surface area is 18 cm^2.

Reaching All Learners

Intervention

Have students draw the surface faces of both of the cube arrangements at the bottom of page 60 and then find their surface areas. They compare answers with those shown on page 60 and are careful about the labels.

Hints and Comments

Overview

Students read the Summary, which reviews the concepts of surface area and volume and the relationships between them.

E Surface Area and Volume

Notes

Provide some solid containers, which students must measure and find the volumes of using the "slice method." These could be common food containers such as salt, cereal, cracker, or pasta boxes. If cones or pyramids are provided, students should be able to tell why they cannot use the "slice method" find these volumes.

Formula for Volume

If an object has a shape that can be cut in slices that all have the same size, you can calculate its volume with the formula:

volume = area of the slice × height

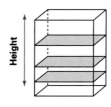

or

volume = area of the base × height

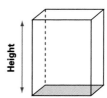

This formula does not work for shapes like cones and pyramids.

Reaching All Learners

Intervention

Have students draw one slice and label the dimensions in their notebook. Then they multiply by the height to find the volume. Calculators may be used.

Hints and Comments

Overview

Students continue reading the Summary, which reviews formulas for finding the volume of shapes.

Surface Area and Volume

Check Your Work

Here are two packages.

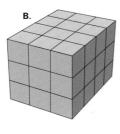

A.   B.

1a Review the way to find volume.

1b Review the way to find surface area.

2 Set up a chart like the one on page 52. Consider having students expand the surface area section.

1. **a.** Which package holds more cubes? How many more cubes?

   b. Which package has more surface area? How much more?

2. **a.** Margaret has 4 different packages. Each package can hold exactly 18 one-centimeter cubes. Describe possible dimensions for Margaret's packages.

   b. What is the surface area for each possible package?

You can buy an aquarium in different shapes.

Here is an L-shaped aquarium with its dimensions.

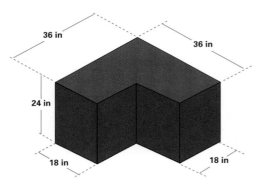

36 in   36 in

24 in

18 in   18 in

3. What is the volume of this aquarium? Show your work.

Assessment Pyramid

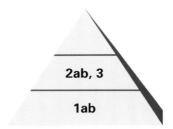

2ab, 3

1ab

Assesses Section E Goals

Reaching All Learners

Intervention

Have students create models with cubes. They divide the model into smaller shapes and find those volumes, then add them together to find the total volume.

Extension

Students may solve problem 1 in two different ways (using the "slice method" or using the formula) to find the volumes. They decide which method is the most sensible and why.

Solutions and Samples

Answers to Check Your Work

1. a. Package A is made out of four layers of eight cubes, so $4 \times 8 = 32$ cubes. Package B is made out of three layers of 12 cubes, $3 \times 12 = 36$ cubes. So Package B holds four more cubes.

   b. The surface area of Package A is: four faces with 8 squares, $4 \times 8 = 32$; and two faces with 16 squares, $2 \times 16 = 32$; so total: $32 + 32 = 64$ squares.

You can draw a net of the wrapping to find this out.

The surface area of Package B is:
$4 \times 12 + 2 \times 9 = 48 + 18 = 66$ squares.
So the surface area of Package B is larger by two squares.

2. a. Answers can vary. If you use only whole numbers, possible dimensions of the packages are:

Package **A:** 3 cm $\times$ 3 cm $\times$ 2 cm

Package **B:** 1 cm $\times$ 2 cm $\times$ 9 cm

Package **C:** 1 cm $\times$ 3 cm $\times$ 6 cm

Package **D:** 1 cm $\times$ 1 cm $\times$ 18 cm

   b. The surface area for the packages from part **a** can be calculated by sketching the net of each package and calculating the area of top and bottom and of the front and back and of the left and right sides.

Package **A:**
$9 \text{ cm}^2 \times 2 + 6 \text{ cm}^2 \times 4 = 18 + 24 = 42 \text{ cm}^2$

Package **B:**
$2 \times 2 \text{ cm}^2 + 2 \times 9 \text{ cm}^2 + 2 \times 18 \text{ cm}^2 = 58 \text{ cm}^2$

Package **C:**
$2 \times 3 \text{ cm}^2 + 2 \times 6 \text{ cm}^2 + 2 \times 18 \text{ cm}^2 = 54 \text{ cm}^2$

Package **D:**
$2 \times 1 \text{cm}^2 + 4 \times 18 \text{ cm}^2 = 74 \text{cm}^2$

3. The volume is 23,328 in³. Sample strategies:

- The L can be reshaped into one rectangular block with a base of 18 in. by (36 + 18) in. and a height of 24 in.

Hints and Comments

Overview

Students use the Check Your Work problems as self-assessment. The answers to these problems are also provided on Student Book pages 78 and 79.

- The L can be split up into a rectangular block with a base of 18 in. by 36 in. and a rectangular block with a base of 18 in. by 18 in. They both have the same height, 24 in.

- The L shape is the difference of a rectangular block with dimensions of base 36 in. by 36 in. and height 24 inches and a rectangular block with dimensions of base 18 in. by 18 in. and height 24 in.

- The L shape can be split into three equal rectangular blocks with a base of 18 in. by 18 in. and a height of 24 in.

Surface Area and Volume

Notes

4 Have students work in groups to solve this problem. Or they could work individually and then compare their answers in the group. It would be interesting to ask students to estimate which container will hold the most trash. Students may do the two rectangular solids first and the cylinder last.

4. Here are three different trash cans. Which one can hold the most trash? Explain how you know.

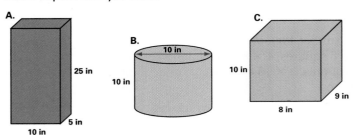

For Further Reflection

Write a letter to someone in your family explaining what perimeter, area, surface area, and volume are and how they are used. You can use pictures in your letter if you think they will help explain the ideas. Describe how the reader can avoid mixing up the ideas and formulas.

Reaching All Learners

Intervention

Some students might find the following instructions for finding volume useful:

• Draw the slice and write its dimensions.

• Then find its area.

• Multiply the area of the slice by the height.

Advanced Learners

Have students draw a triangular-shaped trash can (triangular prism) that can hold the most trash, show its dimensions, and figure its volume.

Solutions and Samples

4. Trash can **A** holds the most trash.

You can justify your answer by showing your calculations for the volume of each.

A. *volume = area of base × height*

$$= (10 \times 5) \times 25$$

$$= 1{,}250 \text{ in}^3.$$

B. Base is a circle with a radius of 5 in.

volume = area of base × height

surface area of the bottom is:

$\pi \times radius \times radius \approx 3.14 \times 25$, which is about 78.5 in^2.

So *volume* $\approx 78.5 \times 10 \approx 785$ in^3.

C. *volume = area of base × height*

volume $= (8 \times 9) \times 10 = 720$ in^3.

Hints and Comments

Overview

Students continue to use the Check Your Work problems as self-assessment. The answers to these problems are also provided on Student Book pages 78 and 79.

Planning

After students complete Section E, you may assign appropriate activities for homework from the Additional Practice section, located on Student Book pages 68 and 69.

Additional Practice

Section Ⓐ The Size of Shapes

1. This square board below costs $20. If it is cut into the pieces shown, how much will each piece cost? Explain your reasoning. What assumptions did you have to make?

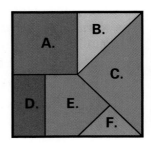

2. What is the area in square units of the shape shown to the right? Show your work.

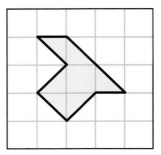

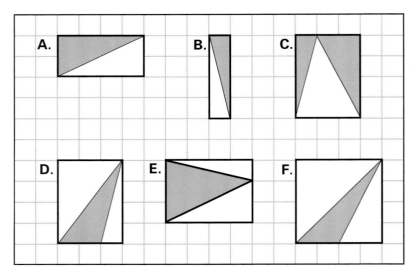

3. A piece of fiberglass that has an area of 4 square units costs $6. How much do the pieces above cost? (The shaded areas represent pieces of fiberglass.)

Section A. The Size of Shapes

1. A. $5.00

  B. $2.50

  C. $5.00

  D. $2.50

  E. $3.75

  F. $1.25

Sample response:

I assumed that the price of each shape matches its area, and that a part is not more expensive because it is a different color.

Strategies will vary. Sample strategy:

The area of part **A** is $\frac{1}{4}$ of the total area of the board, so part **A** will cost $\frac{1}{4}$ of $20, or $5.

The area of part **B** is $\frac{1}{2}$ of the area of part **A**, so part **B** will cost $2.50.

The area of part **C** is twice as large as that of part **B**, so part **C** will cost $5;

The area of part **D** is $\frac{1}{2}$ of the area of part **A**, so part **D** will cost $2.50.

The area of part **F** is $\frac{1}{2}$ of the area of part **B**, so part **F** will cost $1.25.

The area of part **E** is equal to the areas of parts **D** and **F**, so part **E** will cost $2.50 + $1.25 = $3.75.

2. The area is four square units.

Strategies will vary. Sample strategy:

There is one whole square in the middle, and the other parts are half squares, there are six of them. Then I calculated: $1 + 6 \times \frac{1}{2} = 1 + 3 = 4$ square units.

3. A. $6

  B. $3

  C. $9

  D. $6

  E. $9

  F. $6

Strategies will vary. Sample strategy for piece **A**:

I found the area of the rectangle by counting the total number of squares in the shape. It has an area of 8 square units. The area of the shaded region (the fiberglass) is one-half the area of the rectangle, so its area is 4 square units. Each piece of fiberglass that has an area of 4 square units costs $6, so piece **A** costs $6.

Section ◆B◆ Area Patterns

1. **a.** On a grid, draw three triangles that have different shapes but the same area and shade them in.

   b. Draw three different parallelograms that all have the same area. Indicate the base and the height measurements for each figure.

2. Find the areas of the following shapes. Use any method.

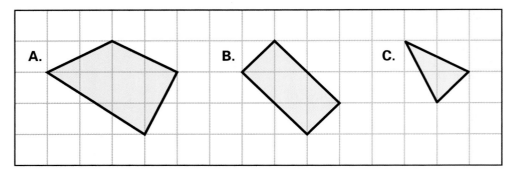

3. Elroy wants to tile his kitchen floor as shown below. He can use large sections of tile, medium sections, or individual tiles. What combinations of sections and individual tiles can Elroy use to cover his floor? Find two possibilities.

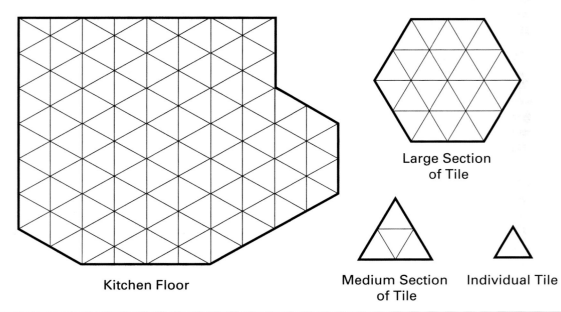

Kitchen Floor

Large Section
of Tile

Medium Section
of Tile

Individual Tile

Section B. Area Patterns

1. a. Drawings will vary. Sample drawings:

b. Drawings will vary. Sample drawings:

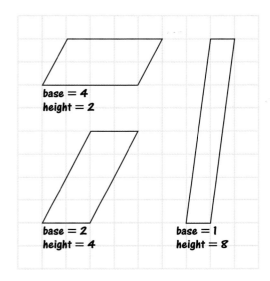

base = 4
height = 2

base = 2
height = 4

base = 1
height = 8

2. A. six square units

B. four square units

C. 1.5 square units

Strategies will vary. Sample strategy for finding the area of shape **C**:

I traced the triangle on another sheet of paper and reshaped the triangle by cutting and pasting parts that would fill the square units on the grid. The triangle has an area of about 1.5 square units.

3. Answers will vary. Sample responses:

Some students may trace the kitchen floor on another sheet of paper and divide it into large and medium sections and individual tiles, as shown here:

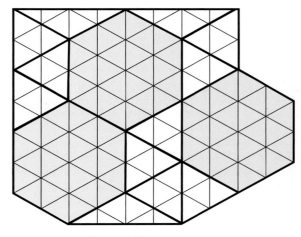

Kitchen Floor

- The kitchen floor (shown above) is made up of 3 large sections and 12 medium sections of tile (three cut in half vertically).

- The kitchen floor is made up of 3 large sections, 9 medium sections (two cut in half vertically), and 12 individual tiles (two cut in half vertically).

- The kitchen floor is made up of 3 large sections, 10 medium sections (three cut in half vertically), and 8 individual tiles.

Additional Practice

Section **C** Measuring Area

1. a. Draw a square. Indicate measurements for the sides so the square encloses an area of 9 ft².

   b. What are the measurements for the sides of this figure in yards? What is the area in square yards?

   c. What are the measurements for the sides of this figure in inches? What is the area in square inches?

2. Convert the following area measurements. Make sketches of rectangles to help you.

   a. 5 m² = _____cm²

   b. 3 ft² = ____in²

   c. 18 ft² = __yd²

   d. 50 cm² = ___mm²

3. The principal's new office, which is 4 m by 5.5 m, needs some type of floor covering. She has the following three choices.

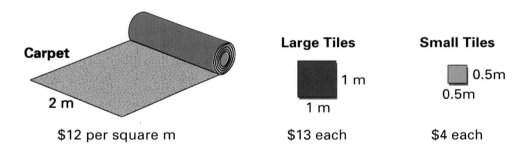

Carpet	Large Tiles	Small Tiles
2 m	1 m × 1 m	0.5m × 0.5m
$12 per square m	$13 each	$4 each

Write a report comparing the three choices. Illustrate your report with sketches of the covered floor for each of the coverings. Be sure to include the cost of each choice. (The carpet and tiles can be cut to fit the shape of the office.)

4. a. Assume that 10 people can stand in one square meter. How big an area is needed for all the students in your class?

   b. How big an area is needed for all the students in your school?

   c. Would it be possible for all the people in your city to stand in your classroom? Explain.

Section C. Measuring Area

1. a. Drawings will vary. Sample drawing:

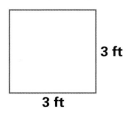

3 ft

3 ft

b. Each side of the square is 1 yd. The area of the square is 1 yd^2.

c. Each side of the square is 36 in. The area of the square is 1,296 in^2.

2. a. 5 m^2 = 50,000 cm^2.

b. 3 ft^2 = 432 in^2.

c. 18 ft^2 = 2 yd^2.

Strategies will vary. Sample strategy.

First I drew a rectangle that has an area of 18 ft^2. Then I divided the rectangle into two squares and labeled the length and width of each square to show their measurements:

18 square feet

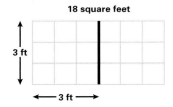

3 ft

3 ft

Then I converted the measurement for the side of each square from feet to yards. Since 3 ft = 1 yd, each side measures 1 yd. So the area of each square is 1 yd × 1 yd, or 1 yd^2, and the area of the rectangle is 2 yd^2.

d. 50 cm^2 = 5,000 mm^2.

3. Reports will vary. Students should include the following information in their reports.

Total area of office: 4 × 5.5 = 22 m^2

Total cost of carpet: $264

Total cost of large tiles: $286

Total cost of small tiles: $352

(Note that four small tiles cover one square meter.)

4. a. The answer depends on the number of students in a class. Sample responses:

- We need an area of 2$\frac{1}{2}$ m^2 since we have 25 students in class.

- We need an area of 2.8 m^2 since we have 28 students in class.

b. The answer depends on the number of students in school. Sample response:

We need an area of 75 m^2 since our school has about 750 students.

c. No. Sample explanation:

We already need 75 m^2 for the students in our school, and our classroom is not much larger than 75 m^2, and there are many more people in our city besides the students in our school.

Additional Practice

Section D Perimeter and Area

1. What are the area and perimeter of each of the following shapes? What do you notice?

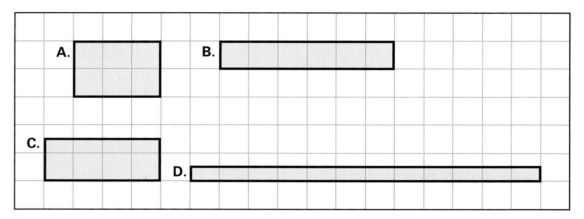

2. **a.** The glass of one of Albert's picture frames is broken. He wants to buy new glass for the picture. The glass must be 12 cm by 15 cm. Glass costs 10 cents per square centimeter. What does Albert have to pay for the glass?

   b. Albert makes an enlargement of the picture: both length and width are now twice as long. How much will the glass for this enlargement cost?

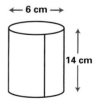

3. Suppose that the container shown above is cut apart into three flat pieces (top, bottom, and side).

   a. Draw the pieces and label their measurements.

   b. What is the area of the top of this container?

   c. What is the circumference of the container?

   d. What is the total surface area of this container? Explain your method.

Section D. Perimeter and Area

1. Perimeter **a** = 10 units; Area **a** = 6 square units.

Perimeter **b** = 14 units; Area **b** = 6 square units.

Perimeter **c** = 11 units; Area **c** = 6 square units.

Perimeter **d** = 25 units; Area **d** = 6 square units.

The area of each rectangle is the same, but each rectangle has a different perimeter.

2. a. $18

Sample calculation:

The area of the glass is $12 \times 15 = 180 \text{ cm}^2$, so this glass will cost $180 \times 10 = 1,800$ cents = $18.

b. $72

Sample explanation:

The 12 cm by 15 cm glass will fit four times on the larger glass. So Albert has to pay four times as much, which is $72.

3. a.

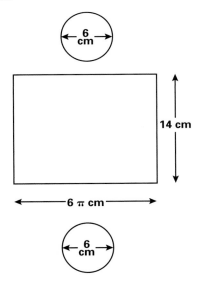

b. Area of top: $\pi \times 3 \times 3 \approx 28.3 \text{ cm}^2$

c. Circumference of container: $6 \times \pi$, or 18.8 cm

d. The surface area is approximately 320 cm^2.

Explanations will vary. Students should add the areas of the top, bottom, and side of the container.

Area top and bottom:

The top and the bottom have the same area (28.3 cm^2).

The side of the container:

The base of this part is equal to the circumference of the container, which is about 18.8 cm. The height is 14 cm, so the area is $18.8 \times 14 \approx 263.2 \text{ cm}^2$.

So the total surface area = $2 \times 28.3 \text{ cm}^2 + 263.3 \text{ cm}^2 \approx 319.8 \text{ cm}^2$.

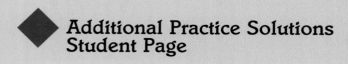 **Additional Practice**

Section Ⓔ Volume and Area

1. Find different-sized boxes using whole numbers as dimensions that will hold exactly 20 one-centimeter cubes. Find as many as you can. Also, find out how much cardboard would be needed to make each box, including the top. Draw a table like the one below for your answers.

Length (in cm)	Width (in cm)	Height (in cm)	Volume (in cm³)	Surface Area (in cm²)
			20	
			20	
			20	
			20	

2. **a.** Name or sketch two objects for which you can use the formula

   volume = area of base × height

   b. Name or sketch two objects for which you cannot use this formula.

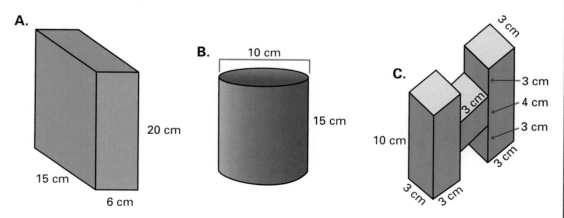

3. Find the volume of each object above. Describe your method.

   a. A box of 15 cm by 6 cm by 20 cm.

   b. A can with a diameter of 10 cm and a height of 15 cm.

   c. An H-shaped block. Base of all parts 3 cm by 3 cm, the height of the standing parts 10 cm, the height of the connecting part 4 cm.

Section E. Volume and Area

1. Sample student response:

Length (in cm)	Width (in cm)	Height (in cm)	Volume (in cm³)	Surface Area (in cm²)
20	1	1	20	82
5	4	1	20	58
5	2	2	20	48
10	2	1	20	64

2. a. A pan, a can, a cereal box, a refrigerator box

b. A pyramid, a tea pot, a bucket, an igloo

3. Volume of **A** = 1,800 cm³

Volume of **B** = 1,177.5 cm³

Volume of **C** = 216 cm³

Sample calculations:

A:
Volume = 6 × 15 × 20 = 1,800 cm³

B:
Area base = 5 × 5 × π ≈ 78.5 cm²
Volume = 78.5 × 15 ≈ 1,177.5 cm³

C:
I split up the shape into three parts.
The volume of the left part is
3 × 3 × 10 = 90 cm³.

The volume of the right part is the same.
The volume of the middle part is
3 × 3 × 4 = 36 cm³.

The total is 90 + 90 + 36 = 216 cm³.

4. On January 27, 1967, Chicago had a terrible snowstorm that lasted 29 hours. Although January in Chicago is usually cold and snowy, 60 cm of snow from one snowstorm is unusual. For three days, the buses stopped. No trains ran. There was no garbage collection or mail delivery. Few people went to work. Most stores were closed. Chicago looked like a ghost town.

a. If the snowstorm lasted 29 hours, why was the city affected for three days?

b. How much is 60 cm of snow?

c. Use the map below to estimate the volume of snow that buried Chicago on January 27, 1967.

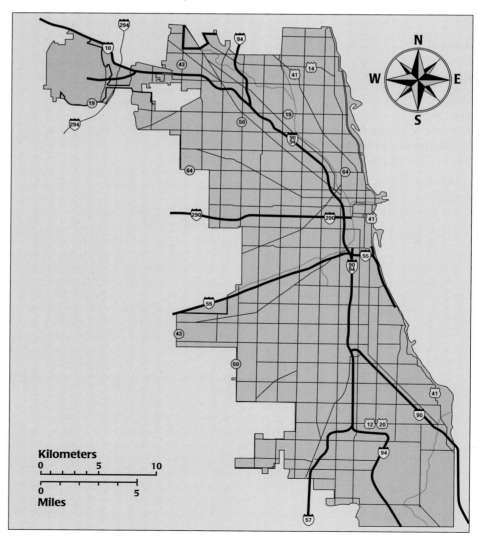

Section E. Volume and Area (continued)

4. a. Answers will vary. Sample response:

Cars and buses can't drive through snow that is 60 cm deep. People had to wait until the snow was removed from the streets.

b. Answers will vary. Sample responses:

- 60 cm of snow is about the length of my leg.
- 60 cm of snow is about the diameter of a car tire.

c. Estimates will depend on the estimated area of Chicago.

Accept student estimates for the area of Chicago from 600 km^2 to 800 km^2.

Accept estimates for the volume of snow from 360,000,000,000,000 cm^3 to 480,000,000,000,000 cm^3.

Sample student reasoning:

The area of Chicago is about 20 km × 40 km. The snow volume is 60 cm by 20 km by 40 km. Change all the dimensions to centimeters (1 km = 100,000 cm) to get 60 cm × 2,000,000 cm × 4,000,000 cm, which is 480,000,000,000,000 cm^3.

Assessment Overview

Unit assessments in *Mathematics in Context* include two quizzes and a Unit Test. Quiz 1 is to be used anytime after students have completed Section B. Quiz 2 can be used after students have completed Section D. The Unit Test addresses most of the major goals of the unit. You can evaluate student responses to these assessments to determine what each student knows about the content goals addressed in this unit.

Pacing

Each quiz is designed to take approximately 25 minutes to complete. The Unit Test is designed to be completed during a 45-minute class period. For more information on how to use these assessments, see the Planning Assessment section on the next page.

Goals	Assessment Opportunities		Problem Levels
• Identify, describe, and classify geometric figures.	Quiz 2	Problems 1c, 4	
• Compare the length and areas of shapes using a variety of strategies and measuring units.	Quiz 1 Quiz 2	Problem 1 Problems 1abc	
• Estimate and compute the areas of geometric figures.	Quiz 1 Quiz 2 Test	Problems 2, 3, 4ab Problems 2a, 4 Problems 1ab	I
• Create and work with tessellation patterns.	Test	Problem 2	
• Use blocks and visualize geometric models to find surface area and volume.	Test	Problems 4a, 5a	
• Understand which units and tools are appropriate to estimate and measure area, perimeter, surface area, and volume.	Quiz 1 Quiz 2 Test	Problems 3, 4ab Problem 1c Problems 2, 4b	
• Understand the structure and use of standard systems of measurement, both metric and customary.	Quiz 2	Problem 2b	II
• Use the concepts of perimeter and area to solve realistic problems.	Quiz 2	Problems 3ab	
• Use various strategies to find the volume of solids.	Test	Problem 3	
• Analyze the effect a systematic change in dimension has on area, perimeter, and volume.	Quiz 2 Test	Problem 3b Problems 3, 5b	III

About the Mathematics

These assessment activities assess the majority of the goals for *Reallotment*. Refer to the Goals and Assessment Opportunities section on the facing page for information regarding the goals that are assessed in each problem. Some of the problems that involve multiple skills and processes address more than one unit goal. To assess students' ability to engage in non-routine problem solving (a Level III goal in the Assessment Pyramid), some problems assess students' ability to use their skills and conceptual knowledge in new situations. For example, in the bird problem on the Unit Test (problem 5b), students must apply their knowledge of general principles of surface area and volume to reason about the surface area of two bird-shaped solids.

Planning Assessment

These assessments are designed for individual assessment; however, some problems can be done in pairs or small groups. It is important that students work individually if you want to evaluate each student's understanding and abilities.

Make sure you allow enough time for students to complete the problems. If students need more than one class session to complete the problems, it is suggested that they finish during the next mathematics class, or you may assign select problems as a take-home activity. Students should be free to solve the problems their own way. Student use of calculators on these assessments is at the teachers' discretion.

If individual students have difficulties with any particular problems, you may give the student the option of making a second attempt after providing him or her a hint. You may also decide to use one of the optional problems or Extension activities not previously done in class as additional assessments for students who need additional help.

Scoring

Solution and scoring guides are included for each quiz and the Unit Test. The method of scoring depends on the types of questions on each assessment. A holistic scoring approach could also be used to evaluate an entire quiz.

Several problems require students to explain their reasoning or justify their answers. For these questions, the reasoning used by students in solving the problems, as well as the correctness of the answers, should be considered in your scoring and grading scheme.

Student progress toward goals of the unit should be considered when reviewing student work. Descriptive statements and specific feedback are often more informative to students than a total score or grade. You might choose to record descriptive statements of select aspects of student work as evidence of student progress toward specific goals of the unit that you have identified as essential.

Use additional paper as needed.

1. Here are maps of two islands, Urba and Cursa. Which one has the larger area?

   Explain your answer.

   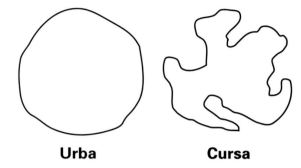

   Urba   **Cursa**

2. Find the area of the rectangle and explain how you found your answer.

   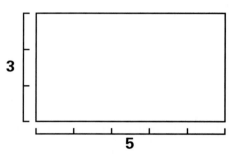

3. Find the area of the triangle. Show how you found your answer.

   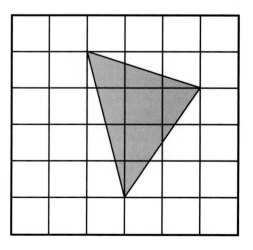

4. The square piece of wood shown below costs $1.00. Calculate
the prices of the other two pieces of wood. Show your work.
(Note: All the pieces have the same thickness.)

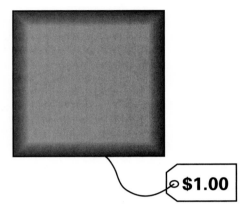

$1.00

a.

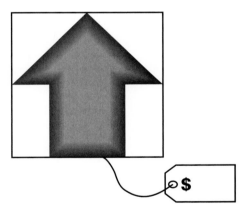

$

b.

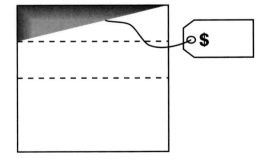

$

Reallotment Quiz 2

Use additional paper as needed.

For this quiz you need a centimeter ruler and centimeter graph paper. You may use a calculator.

1 a. How many centimeters (cm) are there in one meter (m)?

b. Make an exact drawing of one square centimeter (cm²).

c. On centimeter graph paper, make a drawing of a shape that is not a square or a rectangle and that encloses exactly 2 cm².

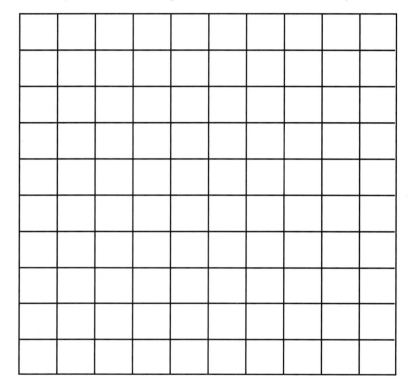

2. A hotel floor will be covered with Italian marble. The marble comes in squares that are exactly 1 m². Leftover pieces will not be wasted; they will be cut to fit spaces where a whole tile will not fit. The dimensions of the rectangle-shaped floor are length $5\frac{1}{2}$ m and width $7\frac{1}{2}$ m.

a. How many square meters (m²) of marble are needed for the floor? Show your work.

b. If the dimensions of the floor were given as $5\frac{1}{2}$ yards long and $7\frac{1}{2}$ yards wide, would the answer to problem 2a (given in square yards) be a larger or smaller area? Explain why.

Mathematics in Context

Miranda has bought a circle-shaped tablecloth for her round coffee table. The diameter of the tablecloth is 1.70 m (or 170 cm). She wants to trim the circumference of the cloth with a braided cord. The trimming cord is sold in pieces rounded to 10 centimeters.

3. a. What length of cord should Miranda buy? Show your work.

b. If the diameter of the tablecloth is twice the diameter of Miranda's table, is the circumference of the tablecloth also twice as big? Explain why or why not.

4. Steve and Miranda bought a new house with a large garden. They want to have a circle-shaped terrace made out of flagstone for dinners outside. The flagstones they would like to use cost $29 per m^2. Steve knows that a terrace built for four people should have a diameter of at least 3 m.

What is the minimum cost of the flagstones to build this terrace?

Use additional paper as needed.

1. Find the area of each shape shown below and explain how you found your answer.

   a.

   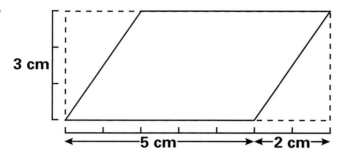

   3 cm

   ←———5 cm———→ ←2 cm→

   b.

   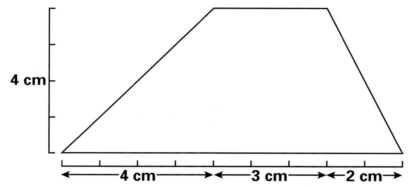

   4 cm

   ←———4 cm———→ ←—3 cm—→ ←2 cm→

2. Look at the tessellation. Find the area of one bird. Explain how you found your answer.

   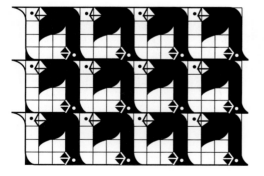

3. Emile used a parallelogram-shaped piece of paper to make the cylinder shown here. Now he wants to make a cylinder with a diameter that has twice the diameter of this one.

What size parallelogram does he need? Explain your answer.

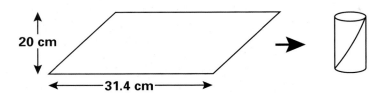

4. A jigsaw puzzle comes in a box (shown on the right) that is 25 cm by 35 cm by 4 cm.

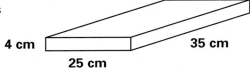

a. You need cartons to ship these boxed puzzles to a toy store. Design a carton that holds exactly 30 of these jigsaw puzzle boxes. Explain your choice.

b. Do you think all possible carton designs will use the same amount of cardboard? Explain your answer.

5. Tim built two "birds" using the same number of cubes for each shape.

a. Does each bird have the same volume? Explain why or why not.

b. Does each bird have the same surface area? Explain why or why not.

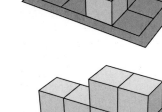

Reallotment Quiz 1
Solution and Scoring Guide

Possible student answer	Suggested number of score points	Problem level
1. Urba has the larger area. Sample explanation: If you trace and cut out the shapes for both islands and place the Cursa shape over the Urba shape, much of the shape for Urba remains uncovered.	**2** (Award 1 point for a correct answer, 1 point for a correct explanation.)	I
2. The area is 15 square units. Sample explanations: • There are three rows with five squares in each row. So there are 3 × 5 = 15 square units. • The area of a rectangle is $A = b \times h$. This rectangle has a base of 5 and a height of 3. So $A = 5 \times 3 = 15$.	**2** (Award 1 point for a correct answer, 1 point for a correct explanation.)	I
3. $5\frac{1}{2}$ square units. Sample explanation: First I drew a rectangle around the shaded triangle. The rectangle measures 3 by 4 unit lengths, so its area is 3 × 4 = 12 square units. I found the areas of the three triangular spaces and added them together. Each of these triangular spaces is half of that of a rectangle. $A = \frac{1}{2} \times 1 \times 4 = 2$ square units $A = \frac{1}{2} \times 3 \times 1 = 1\frac{1}{2}$ square units $A = \frac{1}{2} \times 3 \times 2 = 3$ square units Then, I subtracted the area of the triangular spaces from the area of the rectangle to find the area of shaded triangle. $A = 12$ square units $- 6\frac{1}{2}$ square units $= 5\frac{1}{2}$ square units	**4** (Award 1 point for a correct answer, 3 points for a correct explanation.)	I

Possible student answer	Suggested number of score points	Problem level
4. a. $0.50. Note that students may use drawings to support their reasoning. Sample explanation: I cut the arrow in half lengthwise, and then I cut those pieces in half crosswise. I taped the two rectangles together to make one square, and I taped the two triangles together to make another square. Each of these small squares is $\frac{1}{4}$ of the original square. The total area is $\frac{1}{4} + \frac{1}{4} = \frac{1}{2}$ of the square. The cost of this piece is $\frac{1}{2} \times \$1.00 = \$0.50$.	**2** (Award 1 point for a correct answer, 1 point for a correct explanation.)	I/II
b. About $0.12 or $0.13. Sample explanations: • Eight of the triangle-shaped pieces will fill the original square. The cost of the triangular shape is $1.00 ÷ 8, which is about $0.12 or $0.13. • The triangle shape covers $\frac{1}{2}$ of $\frac{1}{4}$ of the square. The size of this piece is $\frac{1}{2} \times \frac{1}{4} = \frac{1}{8}$. The cost is $\frac{1}{8} \times \$1.00$, or about $0.12 or $0.13.	**2** (Award 1 point for a correct answer, 1 point for a correct explanation.)	I/II
Total score points	**12**	

Reallotment Quiz 2
Solution and Scoring Guide

Possible student answer	Suggested number of score points	Problem level
1. a. 100	1	I
b. Check dimensions of the square. The length width should be exactly 1 cm.	1	I
c. Different shapes are possible: a triangle, a parallelogram, and so on. Check for accuracy.	2	I
2. a. Note that students may use a drawing to support their reasoning. $41\frac{1}{4}$ m² of marble is needed. $5\frac{1}{2} \times 7\frac{1}{2} = 5 \times 7 + 5 \times \frac{1}{2} + 7 \times \frac{1}{2} + \frac{1}{2} \times \frac{1}{2} = 35 + 2\frac{1}{2} + 3\frac{1}{2} + \frac{1}{4} = 41\frac{1}{4}$	2 (Award 1 point for a correct answer, 1 point for a correct calculation.)	I
b. The area would be smaller. Sample explanation: A yard is a little bit shorter than a meter, so a square yard is less than a square meter. That means the area of the floor would be smaller.	2 (Award 1 point for a correct answer, 1 point for a correct calculation.)	II
3. a. Miranda should buy 540 cm of cord. Sample work: The circumference (C) of the cloth with diameter d is: $C = \pi \times d$ or $C = 2 \times \pi \times r$ (r is the radius of the circle) $C = \pi \times 170$ cm ≈ 534 cm The length of the cord she should buy has to be rounded up to 540 cm.	3 (Award 1 point for a correct formula, 1 point for a correct circumference, 1 point for correct student work.)	II
b. Yes. Sample explanations: • If you multiply a length times two and then multiply by π, the answer is twice the original answer. • I calculated $C = \pi \times 2 \times 170 = 1,068$—twice the original answer.	2 (Award 1 point for a correct answer, 1 point for a correct explanation.)	II/III

Possible student answer	Suggested number of score points	Problem level
4. Accept answers between $200 and $205. Students may estimate. Sample work: The area (A) of a circle with diameter 3, or radius 1.5 is: $A = \pi \times r \times r$, so $A = \pi \times 1.5 \text{ m} \times 1.5 \text{ m} \approx 7.07 \text{ m}^2$, or about 7 m^2. 1 m^2 costs $29, so $7.07 \times \$29 = \$205$, or $7 \times \$29 = \$203$.	**4** (Award 1 point for a correct formula, 1 point for a correct radius, 1 point for a correct area, 1 point for correct work.)	I
Total score points	**17**	

Reallotment Unit Test
Solution and Scoring Guide

Possible student answer	Suggested number of score points	Problem level
1. a. 15 cm². Sample explanations: • The area of a parallelogram is A = b × h. This parallelogram has a base of 5 cm and a height of 3 cm, so A = 5 × 3 = 15 (cm²). • I reshaped the parallelogram into a rectangle by cutting off a triangle from one side and pasting it onto the other side. The rectangle is the same size as the parallelogram. Since its area is 15 cm², the area of the parallelogram must also be 15 cm². • I found the area of the broken line rectangle: (7 × 3 = 21 cm²). Then I found the areas of the two triangles: (2 × $\frac{1}{2}$ × 2 × 3 = 6 cm²). Next I subtracted the area of the triangles from the area of the broken line rectangle to find the area of the parallelogram: 21 cm² − 6 cm² = 15 cm².	**2** (Award 1 point for a correct answer, 1 point for a correct explanation.)	I
b. 24 cm². Sample explanations: • First I divided this shape into three parts (labeled them a, b, and c) and found the area of each part. Then I added the areas of the three parts to find the whole area. Area of a = $\frac{1}{2}$ × 4 × 4 = 8 cm². Area of b = 3 × 4 = 12 cm². Area of c = $\frac{1}{2}$ × 2 × 4 = 4 cm². Total area is 8 + 12 + 4 = 24 cm². • I found the area of the rectangle enclosing the shape (4 × 9 = 36 cm²) and subtracted the area of the triangle on the left ($\frac{1}{2}$ × 4 × 4 = 8 cm²) and the triangle on the right ($\frac{1}{2}$ × 2 × 4 = 4 cm²) so that A = 36 − 8 − 4 = 24 cm².	**3** (Award 1 point for a correct answer, 2 points for a correct explanation.)	I
2. 8 square units. Sample explanations: • Two birds cover an area of 16 square units. So one bird covers half of that, or 8 square units. • There are 16 × 12 = 192 square units in the tessellation. There are 24 birds (12 white and 12 black birds). There are 192 ÷ 24 = 8 square units per bird.	**2** (Award 1 point for a correct answer, 1 point for a correct explanation.)	I/II

Possible student answer	Suggested number of score points	Problem level
3. Base is 62.8 cm and height is 20 cm. Sample explanation: The height stays the same. The base of the parallelogram represents the circumference of the cylinder. The formula for circumference is $C = \pi \times d$. If d (the diameter) doubles, the circumference also doubles. So the new circumference is 2×31.4 cm $= 62.8$ cm.	**3** (Award 1 point for each correct dimension, 1 point for a correct explanation.)	II
4. a. Designs will vary. Sample response: My carton measures 35 cm by 50 cm by 60 cm. Two puzzle boxes fit side by side in one layer, which measures 35 centimeters by (25 + 25) cm by 4 cm. Because there are two puzzles in each layer, the box needs to hold $30 \div 2 = 15$ layers. Since each layer is 4 cm tall, the box is 4 cm $\times$ 15 $= 60$ cm tall. Other possible designs for rectangular cartons include: Length Width Height 35 cm 25 cm 120 cm 70 cm 25 cm 60 cm 105 cm 25 cm 40 cm 35 cm 75 cm 40 cm	**3** (Award 1 point for a correct answer, 2 points for a correct explanation.)	I
b. No. Explanations will vary. Sample explanation: For example, a carton measuring 35 cm by 25 cm by 120 cm will take 16,150 cm^2 of cardboard to make. A carton measuring 70 cm by 25 cm by 60 cm needs 14,900 cm^2 of cardboard.	**2** (Award 1 point for a correct answer, 1 point for a correct explanation.)	II
5. a. Yes, each "bird" has the same volume because each cube has the same volume, and each shape has the same number of cubes.	**2**	I
b. No, the surface area is different for each shape. Sample explanation: The number of faces in front and back are equal for each bird since the same number of cubes is used (8 + 8 = 16 faces). The number of faces around the birds is different. I counted 18 faces for the "flamingo" and 14 faces for the "sitting duck."	**2** (Award 1 point for a correct answer, 1 point for a correct explanation.)	III
Total score points	**19**	

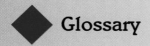

Glossary

Glossary

The Glossary defines all vocabulary words indicated in this unit. It includes the mathematical terms that may be new to students, as well as words having to do with the contexts introduced in the unit. (Note: The Student Book has no Glossary. Instead, students are encouraged to construct their own definitions, based on their personal experiences with the unit activities.)

The definitions below are specific for the use of the terms in this unit. The page numbers given are from the Student Books.

area (p. 3) the number of measuring units needed to cover a shape

base (p. 19) the width of the bottom of a figure

centimeter (p. 25) the hundredth part of a meter, approximately equal to 0.39 inch

circumference (p. 41) the perimeter of a circle

contiguous (p. 7) physically connected (as in the 48 contiguous states of the United States)

diagonal (p. 15) a line segment connecting two nonadjacent corners of a figure

diameter (p. 41) the length of a line segment through the center of a circle ending at its circumference on both sides

equilateral triangle (p. 41) a triangle with equal side lengths and equal angle measures

height (p. 19) the vertical distance from the bottom to the top of a geometric figure or solid

hexagon (p. 41) a six-sided polygon

kilometer (p. 25) a metric unit of length equal to 1,000 meters and approximately equal to 0.62 mile

measuring unit (p. 3) a specific amount used to measure size, either standard, such as an inch or a centimeter, or nonstandard, such as the length of a paper clip

meter (p. 25) a metric unit of length equal to 100 centimeters and equal to approximately 39 inches

net (p. 49) a flat (two-dimensional) pattern that can be cut and folded into a three-dimensional shape

parallelogram (p. 15) a quadrilateral with opposite sides that are parallel

perimeter (p. 38) the distance around a shape

polygon (p. 59) a closed plane figure bounded by straight line segments

quadrilateral (p. 15) a four-sided polygon

radius (p. 43) the length of a line segment between the center of a circle and its circumference

rectangle (p. 15) a parallelogram with four equal angles (all of 90 degrees)

reallotment (p. 6T) the reshaping of a figure to form a new figure in which the area is not changed

regular (p. 41) having equal sides and equal angles

reshape (p. 16) to transform a shape by cutting and pasting

slice (p. 56) a cross-section of a solid

surface area (p. 49) the number of measuring units needed to cover the exterior region of an object

tessellation (p. 4) a repeating pattern with no open spaces that completely covers a shape

triangle (p. 20) a three-sided polygon

volume (p. 49) the amount of space that a three-dimensional figure occupies

BRITANNICA

Mathematics in Context

Blackline Masters

Dear Family,

Your child is about to begin the *Mathematics in Context* unit *Reallotment*. Below is a letter to your child describing the unit and its goals.

This unit introduces the term *reallotment*, which means the reshaping of a figure to form a new figure with the same area as the original. Reallotment often makes it easier to find and compare the areas of different shapes.

You can help your child relate the class work to his or her own life through a variety of at-home activities. You might ask your child to figure out a way to compare the areas of your living room and dining room to see which has the larger area.

You might also ask your child to estimate the cost of installing a fence to enclose your property or to estimate the cost of installing new carpet in the family room.

Students are introduced to tessellations, as shown in the bottom picture of the Student Letter. You might encourage you child to look for tessellation patterns in your home, neighborhood, or local area. You could also ask your child to draw some creative tessellation designs and explain what the repeating pattern is in each design.

Have fun helping your child make these connections between mathematics and the real world!

Sincerely,

The Mathematics in Context Development Team

Dear Student,

Welcome to the unit *Reallotment*.

In this unit, you will study different shapes and how to measure certain characteristics of each. You will also study both two- and three-dimensional shapes.

You will figure out things such as how many people can stand in your classroom. How could you find out without packing people in the entire classroom?

You will also investigate the border or perimeter of a shape, the amount of surface or area a shape covers, and the amount of space or volume inside a three-dimensional figure.

How can you make a shape like the one here that will cover a floor, leaving no open spaces?

In the end, you will have learned some important ideas about algebra, geometry, and arithmetic. We hope you enjoy the unit.

Sincerely,

The Mathematics in Context Development Team

Field A

Field B

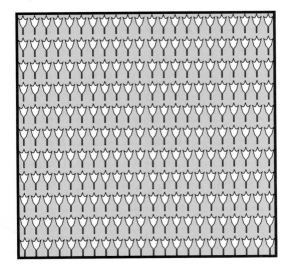

Field C

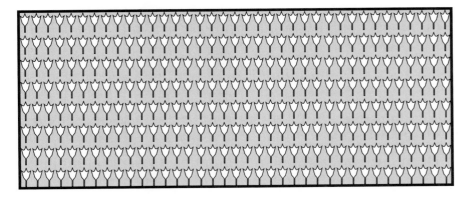

Student Activity Sheet 2

Use with *Reallotment*, page 2.

Name ______________________________

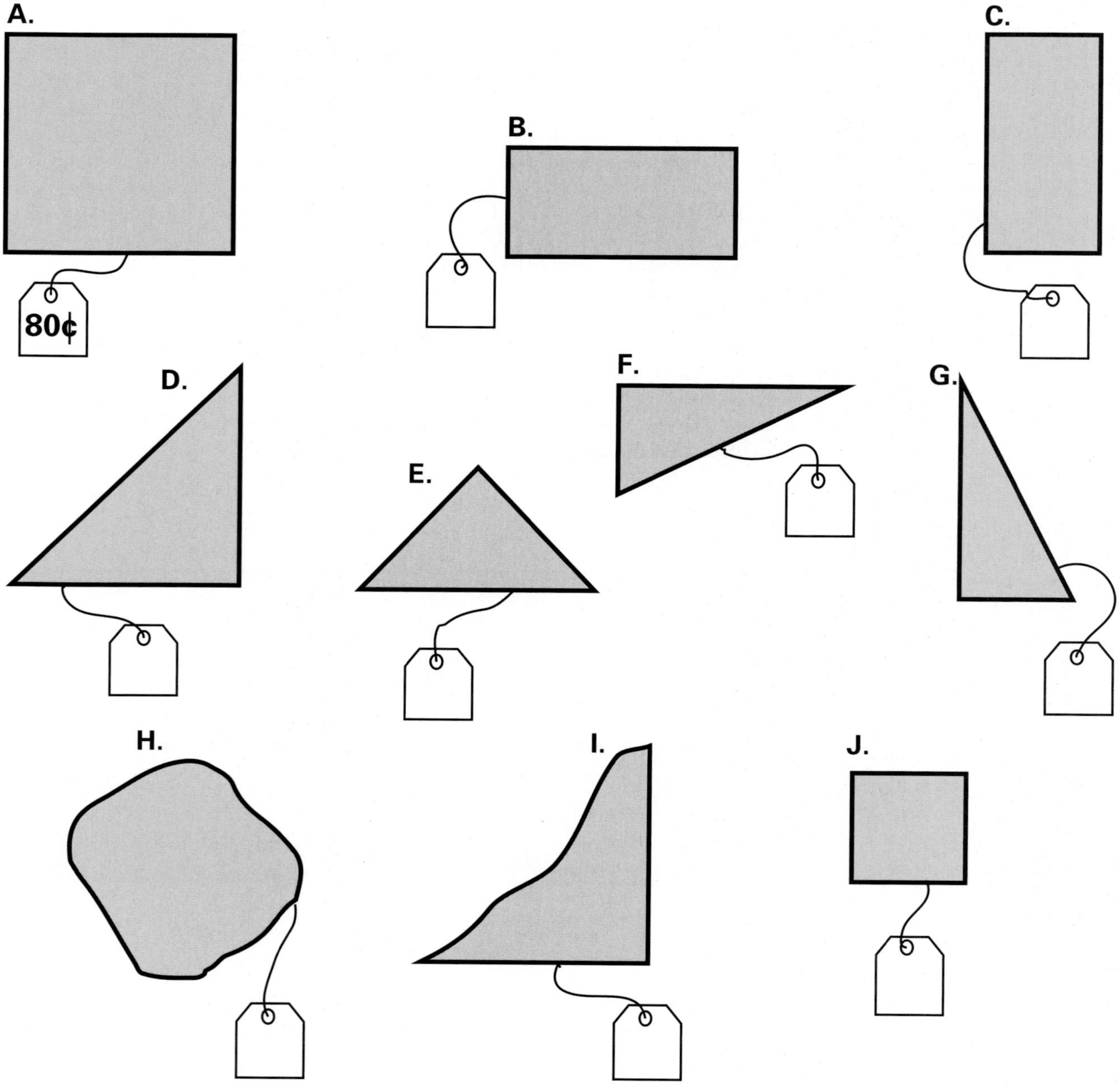

A.

$5

B.

C.

D.

E.

F.

G.

K.

H.

I.

J.

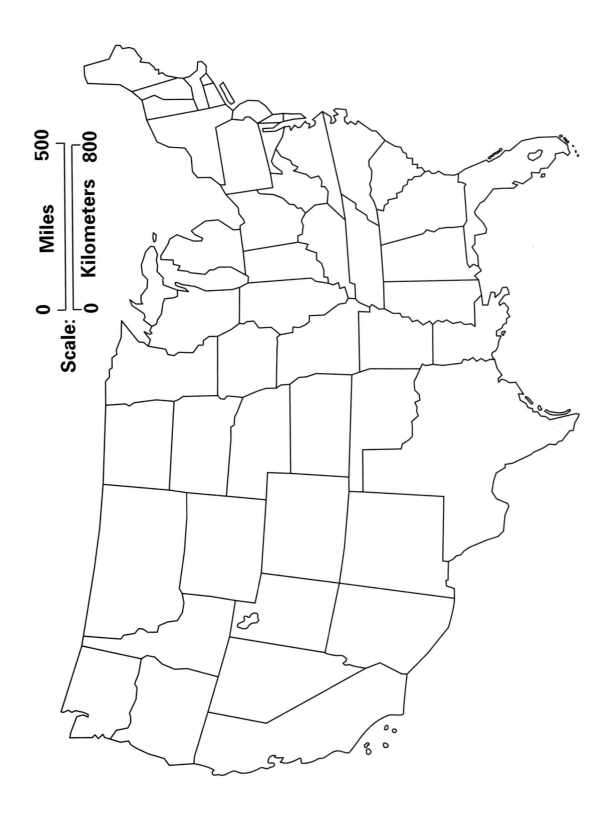

13. **a.** Which island is bigger? How do you know?
    b. Estimate the area of each island in square units.

Space Island

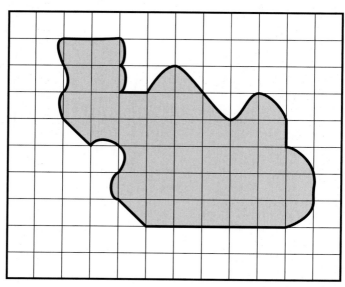

Fish Island

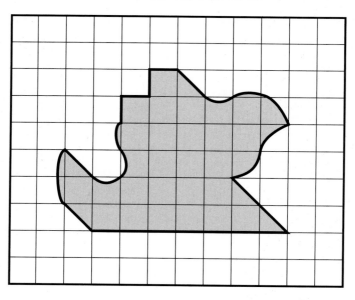

14. What is the area of each of the shaded pieces? Give your answers in square units. Be prepared to explain your reasoning.

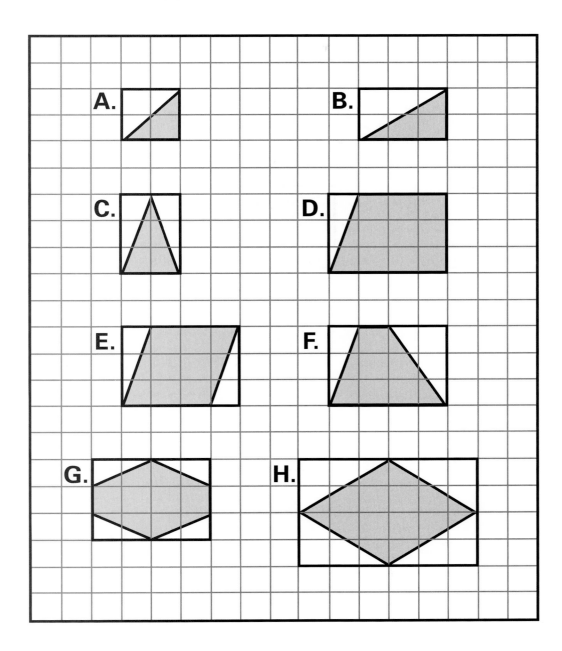

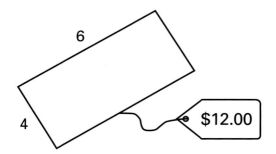

A.
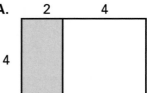

B.
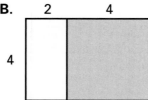

C.
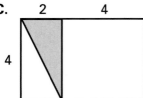

D.
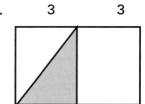

E.
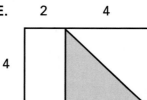

F.
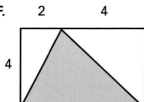

G.
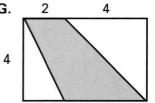

H.
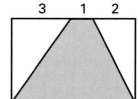

I.
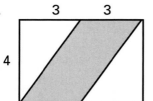

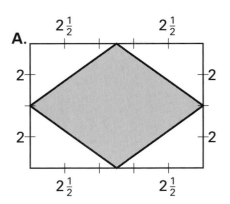

A.

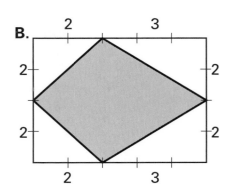

B.

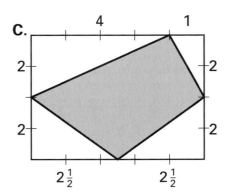

C.

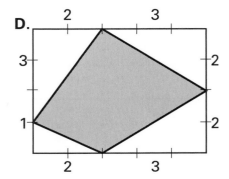

D.

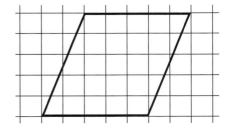

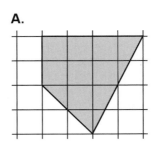

A.

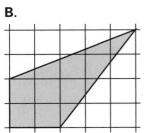

B.

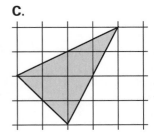

C.

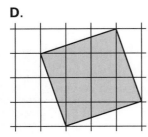

D.

Student Activity Sheet 10
Use with *Reallotment*, page 33.

Name ________________________________

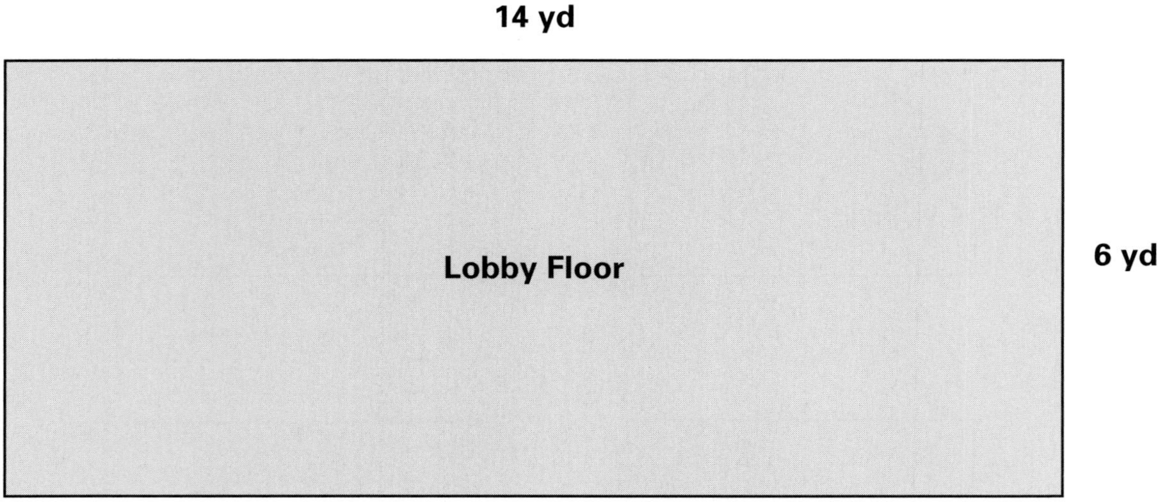
14 yd
Lobby Floor
6 yd

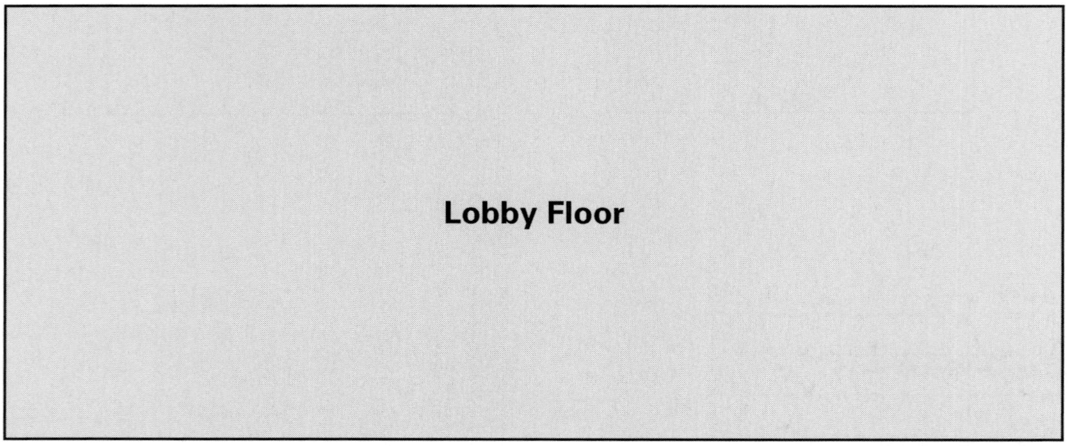
Lobby Floor

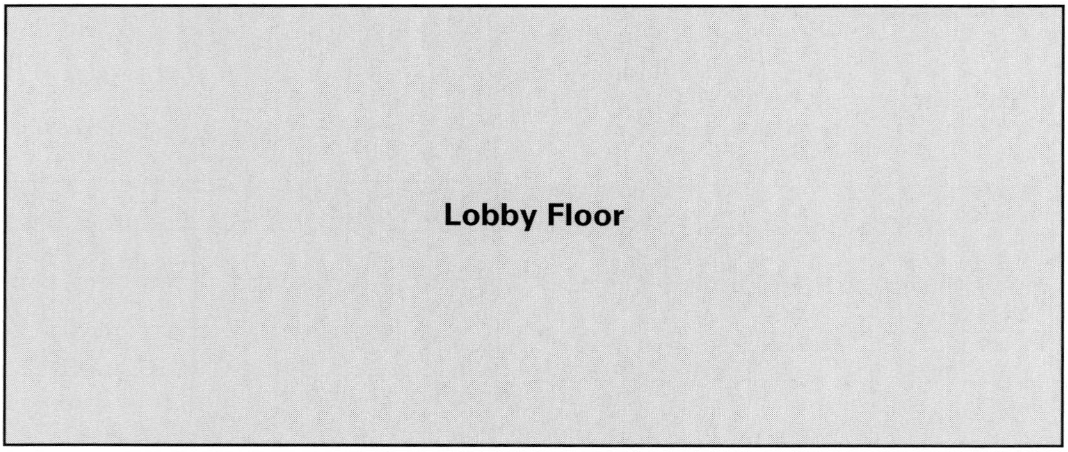
Lobby Floor

Name ______________________________

Student Activity Sheet 11

Use with *Reallotment*, page 33.

Carpet A
4 yd

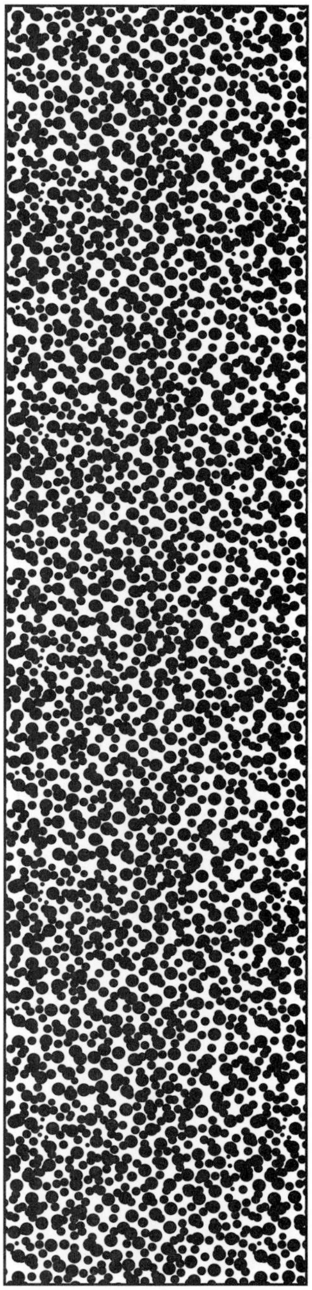

Carpet B
3 yd

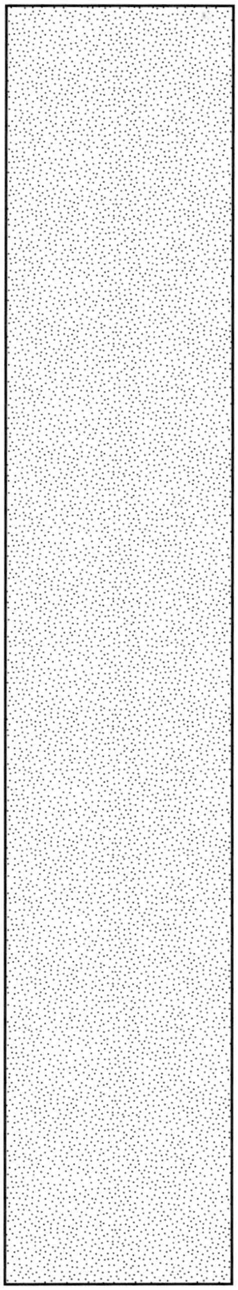

Vinyl
5 yd

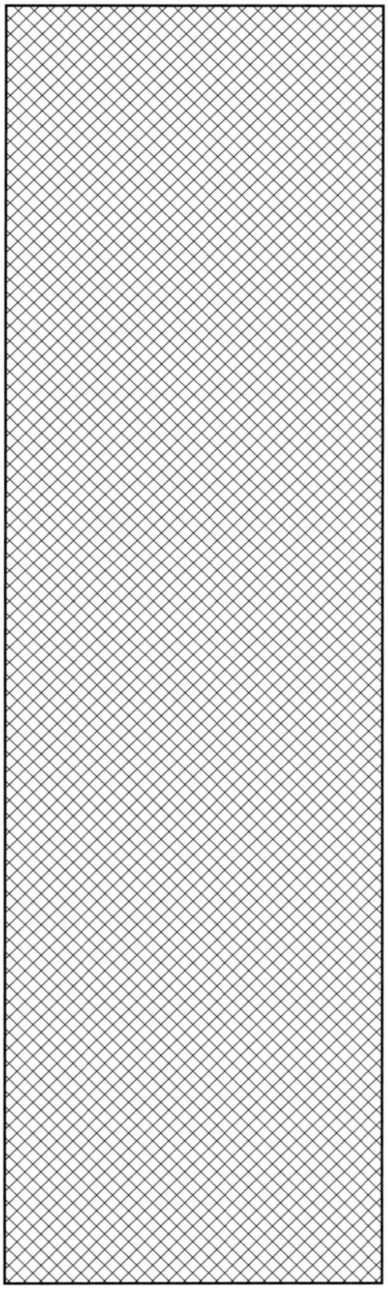

1. a. How many hexagonal tiles were used to create this walkway?

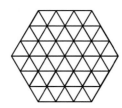

One hexagonal tile.

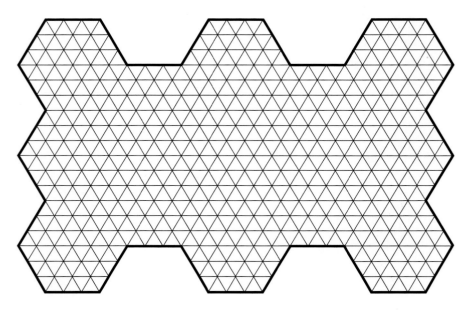

Main Walkway

Estimating the Circumference

	Using 1-cm Triangles	Using 2-cm Triangles	Using 3-cm Triangles	Using 4-cm Triangles
Diameter of Circle				
Perimeter of Hexagon				
Approximate Circumference of Circle				
Perimeter of Square				

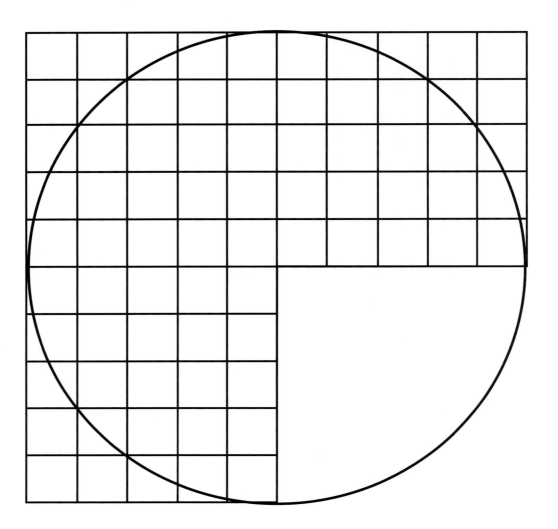

All of the parallelograms below enclose the same area.

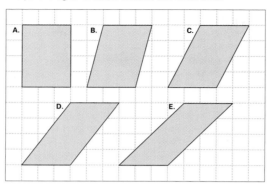

5. **a.** In addition to having the same area, how are all the parallelograms shown here alike?

   b. Describe how each of the parallelograms **B–E** could be transformed into figure **A**.

6. How can your method be used to find the area enclosed by any parallelogram?

In Section A, you learned to **reshape** figures. You cut off a piece of a shape and taped that same piece back on in a different spot. If you do this, the area does not change.

Here are three parallelograms. The first diagram shows how to transform the parallelogram into a rectangle by cutting and taping.

7. Copy the other two parallelograms onto graph paper and show how to transform them into rectangles.

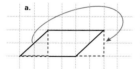 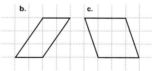

8. Calculate the area of all three parallelograms.

Hints and Comments
(continued from page 16T)

Comments About the Solutions

7. This problem is designed to help students realize that every parallelogram can be transformed into a rectangle with the same area. Some students may need to cut and paste to develop this connection. Allow students to use rulers to draw the diagonals.

   It might be instructive to show how a parallelogram can be copied on graph paper using a counting strategy.

For example, for the parallelogram in problem 7a:

- first locate the lower, left corner point;
- draw a dot where two grid lines cross;
- go from that dot four to the right and place the second dot;
- then go two to the right and two up to place the third dot;
- go four to the left and place the fourth dot; and
- connect the dots.

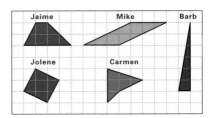

Jaime, Mike, Jolene, Carmen, and Barb drew these shapes.

b. Did they all draw a shape with an area of five square units? Explain why or why not.

c. Draw two triangles that have an area of five square units.

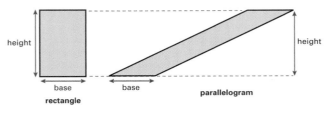

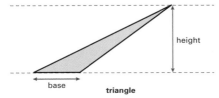

You worked with three shapes in this section. When you describe a rectangle, parallelogram, or triangle, the words **base** and **height** are important. The base describes how wide the figure is. The height describes how tall it is.

13. a. Use the words *base* and *height* to describe ways to find the areas of rectangles, parallelograms, and triangles. Be prepared to explain why your ways work.

   b. Check whether your description for finding the area works by finding the area for some of the rectangles, parallelograms, and triangles in problems you did earlier in this section and in Section A.

   c. Draw a triangle with base 4 and height 2. Now draw a triangle with base 2 and height 4. What observations can you make?

Hints and Comments
(continued from page 19T)

Comments About the Solutions

13. If students have difficulty seeing that the parallelogram on page 19 of the Student Book has the same area as the rectangle, you may show how the parallelogram can be transformed into the rectangle on the overhead using the same procedure as shown on page 17 of the Student Book.

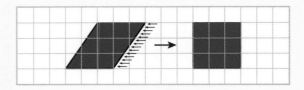

b. To save time, you may assign groups of students to check one of each shape. Be sure students mention the page number and problem number of the shape they checked.